More S

more SALT than PEPPER

Dropping Anchor with

KARAN THAPAR

Illustrations by Jayanto Banerjee

HarperCollins *Publishers* India
a joint venture with

New Delhi

First published in India in 2009 by
HarperCollins *Publishers* India
a joint venture with
The India Today Group

ISBN: 978-81-7223-776-9

2 4 6 8 10 9 7 5 3 1

Grateful acknowledgement is made to the *Hindustan Times*, where these
columns originally appeared.

HarperCollins *Publishers*
A-53, Sector 57, NOIDA, Uttar Pradesh – 201301, India
77-85 Fulham Palace Road, London W6 8JB, United Kingdom
Hazelton Lanes, 55 Avenue Road, Suite 2900, Toronto, Ontario M5R 3L2
and 1995 Markham Road, Scarborough, Ontario M1B 5M8, Canada
25 Ryde Road, Pymble, Sydney, NSW 2073, Australia
31 View Road, Glenfield, Auckland 10, New Zealand
10 East 53rd Street, New York NY 10022, USA

Typeset in 11/15 Minion Pro
Jojy Philip New Delhi 110015

Printed and bound at
Thomson Press (India) Ltd.

For Mummy, with love

Contents

Preface

The publication of a collection of my 'Sunday Sentiments' columns for the *Hindustan Times* should be an occasion for celebration. However, it fills me with a measure of dread and even a certain queasiness. Though, if you think about it, that shouldn't come as such a big surprise.

Wouldn't you dread the prospect of re-reading in bound book form pieces that were hurriedly dashed off to meet newspaper deadlines? Do they withstand a second outing? Worse, do they betray a shallowness or, God forbid, a silliness, that went unnoticed in the rush to read the paper on a Sunday morning but now, as you encounter them in these pages, is inescapable and, possibly, unforgivable?

And queasiness? Well, whilst it's no doubt a delight to see something you've written in print, wouldn't you feel a little bilious if you suddenly found yourself holding so many pieces at one time? As the saying goes, too much of a good thing can be bad for one!

So, if you venture beyond this page, let me, in advance, offer an apology if my fear or anxiety proves accurate. But if you do, let me also explain my approach to the writing of these columns. It might help you understand them – and, who knows, me? – a little better.

These are not political columns. On the contrary, I tried hard not to reveal my own political views and, certainly, my political preference. As a television current affairs anchor, I believe it's important that the audience should not know my own political position. Otherwise they will judge my interviews in the light of what they believe is my acknowledged viewpoint. So to ensure that image of neutrality I've struggled – hopefully successfully – to keep narrow politics and political affiliation out of these columns.

However, this does not mean that I've avoided political subjects. Simply that I've tried to be analytical and not merely to opine. But if on occasion my analysis reveals a personal standpoint I won't run away from any conclusions you draw. I may disagree but I accept your right to infer and deduce.

More importantly, I believe there's more to life than politics. These columns attempt to embrace that wider and far more interesting part of our existence. The peculiar or the inexplicable, the droll and the ironic, the ugly, even the horrifying, and the humdrum, the forgotten and, of course, the erroneous as well as the mistaken have often caught my attention and tickled my fancy. On a reflective Sunday morning, they deserve as much – if not more – attention than the political issues that impose themselves on us through the week.

A lot of the columns are about what I call 'Me and Mine'. The world I live in and the characters who people it often feature in the stories I tell. They appear as I know them – chatty, casual, sometimes admonishing, frequently joking, always warm and friendly. I've never been hesitant about including them. And over the last twelve years they've become a central part of 'Sunday Sentiments'.

Often the columns are about small, seemingly insignificant but, actually, substantial lessons that I've learnt. Though related anecdotally, there is a moral, simple but telling, that is embedded in each one. In a sense these have become precepts I personally observe – or, at least, try to.

But there is another side to me that these columns will also reflect. I admire outspoken people, I enjoy the company of the charming, the sight of the well-dressed and the humour of the naturally witty. In other words, I like people who stand out and impress me. And I've often written about them.

Not surprisingly, many of the columns are personal. Not just in content but also in tone. Much of the time they are an attempt to talk directly to the reader. Almost a chat, you could say. But that's what I always wanted. My aim was to make these columns different. Not didactic, certainly not arcane and never formidable, but always accessible and friendly.

Finally, on each occasion, my conscious attempt has been to entertain. I believe a piece of writing needs to be readable to be read. Therefore, the first duty of the author is to be interesting. If he or she cannot manage that, the reader has every right to turn the page and skip to another article or, if it's a book, leave it idling on a shelf.

This is not to suggest that content is unimportant but that if you have things to express without the necessary style for doing so, you will remain unread.

Consequently, I don't mind being wrong, or courting controversy, or inflaming passions but I would hate to be boring.

Now, if you want, read on and see if I've correctly understood myself and my columns or if I've misled you with my own false consciousness!

New Delhi, Karan Thapar
24 July 2009

PART I

Ties that Bind

Chapter 1

'Is Your Wife at the Party?'

'Why aren't the two of you living together?'

A Time for Father Terry

It's as clear in my memory as if it happened yesterday. But in fact I first met Father Terry Gilfedder twenty-five years ago. It was the late summer of 1982 and Nisha and I were preparing for our marriage. As a Catholic she wanted a proper church wedding and whilst I agreed, I was irritated by the need to meet the local parish priest for a set of three 'tuitions'. But there was no way out. The nearest church, St. Mary Magdalene's in Northumberland Avenue, would only marry Nisha to a non-Christian if this requirement was complied with.

So one Saturday in September, around 6 in the evening, Nisha and I knocked on Father Terry's door. He was sitting at his desk, his spectacles perched at the end of his nose. We settled into an old, well-worn leather sofa on the opposite side of the small room. Outside it was unusually warm, inside the atmosphere felt frosty. I was itching for a fight.

'Sherry?' The offer took me by surprise. 'I don't know about you two, but I'm rather partial to the stuff.'

It was Tio Pepe, my favourite, but in those days a rarity in London. Father Terry was a man of discerning taste. I found myself discussing the US Open Tennis, the Nottinghill Carnival, Rushdie's *Midnight's Children* – in fact, anything but our forthcoming marriage or what religion our unborn children would follow.

Father Terry would top up our glasses and steer the conversation. He enjoyed an argument and held his own comfortably. The hour passed swiftly and enjoyably. Having agreed to meet the next week, we got up to leave. We were at the door when Father Terry stopped us.

'There's a question I'd like you to think about.' A hint of a smile played on his large round face. His eyes were looking straight at us. 'Why aren't the two of you living together?'

I'm not sure if the blood drained from our faces but we were speechless and stunned. The truth is Nisha and I were living together but had deliberately given Father Terry different addresses to hide the fact. He had guessed and this was his way of saying it didn't matter.

Father Terry became a close friend. At a rehearsal two nights before our wedding, he suggested one of the readings should be from the Gita and asked me to choose. On the day when I revealed I had failed to pick a passage, he slapped me on the back and laughed: 'I knew that would happen so I've chosen something myself.' It was from Khalil Gibran's *The Prophet*.

Nisha had hoped for a full communion mass and Father Terry agreed, overlooking the fact that the groom was not a Christian. But it was his sermon that captured attention. He didn't pontificate about hell and damnation or God and his goodness. He spoke, as he put it, of 'three little words': I love you.

'Karan and Nisha,' he said, 'remember love joins "I" and "you" but it can also separate. The day you forget you're two different individuals, that bond can become a divide.'

It was a warm, simple, heartfelt message. More a fireside chat than a formal sermon. But it's stayed seared in my memory for a quarter century.

Six years later, as Nisha lay dying with moments to go before the life support was switched off, Father Terry was at her bedside. He gave her the last sacrament but also encouraged Mummy to whisper Hindu prayers in her ear. Then he stood beside me as the machines slowly, painfully, flickered to a close and Nisha's life ebbed away.

Terry Gilfedder is the only Christian priest I've known. He was an unusual man but a great person. I think of him each time I read of attacks on Christians in Orissa and Karnataka. I'm confident he would have found the words to heal bruised hearts. And, no doubt, his sherry would have helped!

I'm sure there are Father Terrys in all faiths. Men of God but also caring, understanding human beings. Today, when we most need them, why are they silent?

9 October 2008

Say It with Flowers

It happened in 1986. It was a crisp sunny Valentine's Day and I remember the brilliance of the bright-blue sky. My desk at London Weekend Television, where I worked, overlooked the Thames and the view that morning was stunning. It was the first Valentine's Day after my wedding that I can remember. Nisha and I had been married three years but the tradition of gifting red roses was not a part of our lives.

Around noon, whilst bantering with friends over coffee, the phone rang. It was the lady from the reception to say someone had delivered a gift and should she send it up. I said she should but even so I was unsuspecting. I assumed it was a book for reviewing or a corporate package from a company about to hold its AGM.

Minutes later an attractive svelte blonde with hair that swayed as she moved sashayed out of the lift and into the office. She paused beside the first desk, bent down to speak and then continued in my direction. Three feet short, she dramatically dropped to her knees, stretched out her right-hand and proffered a single red rose.

'From a secret admirer,' she said deliberately loudly. 'She wants you to know she loves you very much.'

Practically everyone on the tenth floor at LWT burst out laughing. I turned beetroot red. But inside I was thrilled. Who could this be? To have an admirer is wonderful, but a secret one who had sent me red roses by special courier on Valentine's Day was almost beyond imagining.

After the teasing and joking ended, I rang Nisha to tell her. She responded with a strange noncommittal silence. I was so wrapped up in my story I failed to notice she wasn't saying very much.

'So, Baba,' she cooed, far too knowingly to be natural. 'You have a secret admirer! Any idea who it might be?'

'Haven't the foggiest,' I responded, still delighted by the mystery.

'Silly boy,' she laughed. Nisha sounded pleased with herself. 'Do you really think there could be two women who love you?'

'Who's the first?' I asked, perplexed.

'Your wife, you fool!'

I was stunned. I thought Nisha would be the last person to send me roses on Valentine's Day. Her gesture had completely taken me in. As I gasped for something to say, she continued: 'See you in the evening and remember you're cooking dinner tonight!'

It's such displays of affection that the RSS seems to be against. That, after all, is the ultimate consequence of its decision to oppose Valentine's Day. According to newspaper reports, their spokesperson has concluded that sending red roses – or other gifts – to people you care for is un-Indian. Perhaps, but is it wrong? And does the RSS fully realize what this objection seems to imply?

In the land of Khajuraho, Konark and the Kama Sutra, the perfection of sex is, undeniably, part of Indian tradition. No one has taken this art to higher levels. Even the RSS cannot deny that – although, like the rest of their countrymen, it's true they've forgotten the valuable lessons our forefathers left behind. Today, Indians might possibly be masters of theory but they are very definitely dreadful practitioners of the art of making love.

Now what the RSS seems to be saying is that sex is Indian but affection and love are not. It's Indian to learn how to kiss and copulate but not how to court and woo. In other words, sex without emotion we accept, but sentiment and affection we reject.

Odd! I thought the West stood for 'wham bam thank you ma'm' whilst Indians believed that sex without love was akin to animal procreation! Suddenly it seems to be the other way round. Should we be grateful to the RSS or have they got it wrong?

I'll let the elders of the Sangh answer that question although I'm keen to know what it will be. Let me instead point out that these views accord most closely with those of the religious establishment in Saudi Arabia. By means of an official fatwa the dour Saudis banned red roses this Valentine's Day. And in case the amorous citizenry thought otherwise most florists chose to stay shut. Reading about this in the *Financial Times*, I couldn't help but groan. The RSS, no doubt, would have smiled. It only proves great minds think alike or …

Would you say the other half of that famous equation fits better?

16 February 2006

Are You Married?

Have you been in one of those situations where the conversation takes a turn of its own? It usually starts with an innocent enquiry, you reply with an equally considerate answer and then suddenly, without anyone knowing how it happened, the person jumps to the wrong conclusion. Or, worse, it becomes horribly embarrassing.

In the early 1990s this sort of thing used to happen a lot when people asked if I was married. I am. But the truth is I am also a widower. Nisha, my wife, died thirteen years ago. But that doesn't undo the marriage. If I had said 'no' that would be a lie. If I had said I was 'a widower' I might embarrass the questioner, who could feel he had accidentally trod on delicate territory. So when the question was popped I simply said 'yes'. Incidentally, that also happened to be how I felt about it emotionally. But the conversation never ended there. That's the problem. Inevitably the outcome would go in the wrong direction.

Let me illustrate.

'Nice to meet you,' the person would begin as I was introduced to a stranger at a party, or as I sat down beside a lady I'd never met before and struggled for something clever to start a conversation.

'Are you married?'

It's the sort of thing most people always asked. At the time I was in my thirties with a head full of relatively black hair and it was, I suppose, a natural question. Now that I'm grey the question feels redundant. Most people assume I am.

Anyway, this is when the problem started. I would answer 'yes'.

'Is your wife at the party?' the person would continue. I'd never know how to reply. 'Yes' would be a lie. 'No' was the truth but it would indubitably lead to further questions about where she was and that, in turn, would only make matters worse. Suddenly I would realize the folly of my first answer. But I'd only said yes to the original question because I did not want to embarrass the person by saying I was a widower. It always makes the questioner feel awkward. After all, polite questions are not supposed to elicit painful memories.

Things are a lot different now that I look visibly too old not to be married. My hair is more salt than pepper, my face has crow's feet – if not reptilian lines – and because people think they know me they also feel my life must conform to the norm they expect of people my age. So they assume I'm married. This is how our conversations now fare.

'Where's your wife?'

It's meant as a pleasant opening gambit. They don't know that she's dead. They'd be horrified to find out. But because they've assumed I'm married they also assume she's around.

Tell me, in my position what would you say? Thirteen years after Nisha's death I feel I can blurt out the truth without feeling pain. Also, since I'm conscious of not wanting to embarrass, I'm aware it's better to be honest at the outset even if that makes for a brief awkward moment.

In fact, I've toyed with several answers. 'She's not here' is one but it doesn't help. People immediately want to know where she is and when they find out they're embarrassed. Another is to say 'I'm no longer married'. But that doesn't help either. The person always wants to know why. The inquisitive think I'm divorced and there's a story to ferret out. The supportive assume I need help. Whilst the solicitous offer to arrange a marriage!

But once – and only because I was a wee bit tight – I answered with the bald, blunt, brutal truth. This is how it went.

'Where's your wife?'

'Dead.'

'What do you mean? When did that happen? Oh God, how terrible! You poor, poor chap.'

The person got into a terrible fluster. In fact, he went beetroot red. I knew I was being heartless but who told him to start by assuming I was married and that my wife must be around? The fault – if that's how I can describe it – was his and I did not feel like pushing myself to give a deceptive but gentle answer. However, after a bit, I decided to soften the blow.

'Don't worry. She died thirteen years ago. You weren't to know.'

It worked. His face broke into a smile. Relief flooded his features as inwardly he excused his own faux pas.

'Well,' he said, his confidence restored. 'Time for round two. I'd try again if I were you. You need a woman by your side as you head for the grave. Your second wife is bound to outlive you. And then she can face the question, "Where's your husband?"'

8 July 2002

Chapter 2

Family Ties

'Daddy's ties were nice but they were almost entirely regimental... But there was one that jumped out at me.'

Baba Gajju and the House of Mewar

Arvind Mewar has just published a sumptuous history of his ancestors. Although a coffee table presentation it's very readable and the pictures are stunning. But it's the little stray facts that I found the most surprising. I had no idea the House of Mewar was the world's longest serving dynasty, although that service surely terminated in 1947, if not earlier when the British Residents muscled in. It was equally eye-opening to find that Maharana Pratap never really defeated the Mughals. I always thought he had and I'm a little sorry to know the truth. But I'm inexplicably thrilled to discover that it was a maharana called Karan who conceived of and started work on the Lake Palace!

My point is that ancestors are a good thing. We all have them though most of us have an unfailing tendency to lose them. Once they disappear into the mists of time they are easily forgotten. Actually, not mine, though the credit for that cannot be claimed by me.

My cousin, Romilla, a historian of some repute, has researched the foundations of the family. We may not stretch as far back as the Suryavanshi Mewars (although their policy of adopting heirs when no bloodline descendent was available does make their family tree look a little contrived) but we do at least make it back to Babar.

The first Thapar – or so Romilla claims – came across with the Great Mughal. The year, I believe, was 1526. His name was Baba

Gajju. What he did in Babar's entourage Romilla has not disclosed. I suspect he was a bootblack but he might even have been a *bhisthi*. Perhaps Gunga Din was one of his great-grandsons! However, family lore maintains he was a noble man. Years ago we used to have great fun about this.

'*Nanaji*,' my nephew Siddo once proclaimed when he was ten, '*Kya mere pad, pad, pad dada* Babar *ke dhobhi the*?'

Had he worn moustaches Daddy's would have bristled. Siddo was his first grandchild but this was a matter of family honour.

'Baby,' he would shout at my sister. 'What is this nonsense you're teaching the boy?'

A decade later, when I got married, my sister Premila told Nisha she ought to name our first son Gajju.

'What sort of name is that?' asked Nisha, blissfully unaware of its significance.

'Ah,' Premila replied. 'Everything flows from him. He's the original wonder responsible for the family chain.'

Thereafter for years the awaited sprog was referred to as Baby Gajju. Perhaps that's why he was never born. Children are deeply sensitive and the prospect of carrying a silly name was probably enough to drive the foetus back into the womb!

In fact it was only for the first few months that the family took seriously Romilla's discovery of our origins. Once the novelty wore off interest started to wane. After all, we weren't maharanas nor did my ancestors influence great decisions. Although in recent times my grandfather was elevated to Diwan Bahadur after independence, that's best forgotten. So, I daresay, none of us is going to publish a history of the family.

Yet few pastimes are more absorbing than rummaging through the family's forgotten closets. Sit down with your parents (or grandparents) and start asking questions. You'll be fascinated by the stories that pop out. Even if you don't publish a history to beat Arvind Mewar's you will find out a lot you never knew. And you'll have a lot of fun too.

17 April 2000

Bim and Bimla

It's odd how you forget your parents were once young. For instance, I regard Mummy as youthful but, in fact, that also emphasizes her age. But the other day I learnt of someone who had a crush on her almost seventy-five years ago! And it happened in the most bizarre sort of way. It's a perfect story for a mid-December Sunday morning.

Three weeks ago a friend of my parents telephoned to say he'd just written a book. You probably know him as Lt. Gen. M.N. Batra. He was, in the 1970s, one of our better directors general of military intelligence. Before that, I'm told, he was a champion boxer. Bishop Cotton would be hard pressed to produce better. However, I have always known him as Uncle Bim. Tall, dapper, frequently smiling and the author of witty middles for The *Times of India*, Uncle Bim is avuncular, hearty and a joy to meet in the corridors of the club. But it never occurred to me to question why everyone calls him Bim. Until, of course, I found out.

It happened like this. I walked into Masi's with Uncle Bim's book tucked under my arm. It's called *In the Middle* and it caught her attention at once.

'What's that?' she asked. Masi is a bit like Bertie Wooster's Aunt Agatha. She has a stentorian voice and is used to being obeyed.

'Oh,' I said, a little taken aback. 'Uncle Bim's book.'

'Show it to me at once.'

I did. Masi looked at the cover and smiled. I watched in silence. She started to chuckle.

'That's just like old Bim.' She was staring at a Sudhir Dar cartoon that bore a remarkable likeness to its inspiration. 'They used to call him Bim Four.'

'Bim Four?'

'And all because of your mother,' Masi continued, ignoring my interruption but also answering it.

'Hang on,' I interrupted again. This was too much for me. 'What does Mummy have to do with Uncle Bim? I thought he was in the army with Daddy.'

'This was long before your mother married your father. She was only a young girl at the time.' And then, after a pause, Masi added, 'I was only four.'

From experience I know you can't hurry my aunt. She likes to tell her stories in her own way. So I waited patiently for her to continue.

'There were four Batra boys at Bishop Cotton. The oldest was Raj. A good-looking lad although not my type. But he couldn't take his eyes off your mother. Wherever Bimla went Raj was sure to follow. So the boys used to call him Bim.'

'But Uncle Bim's name is Mohinder?' Masi's story didn't seem to add up.

'Patience,' Masi admonished and I lapsed into silence. I'm a lamb in her presence.

'Raj had three brothers – or cousins – or whatever.' She dismissed the relationship with a vigorous sweep of her hand. 'They were called Bim Two, Bim Three and Bim Four. Mohinder was Bim Four.'

Masi's story went no further but the next morning I rang Uncle Bim for verification. I half expected a loud laugh and a firm denial. What I got instead went well beyond corroboration.

'Good grief,' he began. 'Your aunt has an amazing memory for her age. Yes, Bim Four I was. But do you know your old Mamu didn't approve of the attention we paid your mother!'

'Really?' This was getting better and better.

'I remember playing *gulli-danda* at your grandparents' place in Simla and Bimla wanted to join in. Gogu refused to let her. Protective little blighter he was. Until, of course, she caught my *gulli*. Well, no one could stop her then!'

Fortified by these stories I decided to accost Mummy. In fact, I relished the prospect. With a big broad smile and a knowing glint in my eyes I approached the subject at our next meeting.

'I've just found out who your boyfriend was!'

'Darling,' she replied, waving her carefully polished nails, 'Which one? I must have had several.'

'Uncle Bim,' I riposted, refusing to be so easily deflated.

'Ah.' Her voice seemed to trail off. 'He used to carry sweets in his pocket. And they were only for me. Of course, he was only ten at the time.'

'And you?'

'I was fourteen.'

I finished Uncle Bim's book at one go that night. It's delightfully written and I recommend it. Now I want to read his autobiography. I wonder what stories he has to relate?

9 December 2004

The Tie that Really Binds

There's nothing I like more than a nice tie. Although I'm proud of my collection of Hermes and Ferragamo they are by no means the only ones I'm fond of. Yet sadly some that I've taken a fancy to have been meant for other people. If that doesn't make immediate sense read on, for in the mystery lies a pretty tale.

In December 1976, a year and a bit after my father's death, I happened to be holidaying in Delhi. Mummy had arranged a small dinner and I was commanded to attend.

'But I have nothing to wear,' I desperately pleaded. I could have added that I had nothing in common with the generals she had invited but I knew that would be brushed aside. So I stuck to the excuse of my supposed sartorial inadequacy.

'Open Daddy's cupboard and take whatever you need,' the mater swiftly responded. 'You won't find better ties than his.'

Now Daddy's ties were nice but they were almost entirely regimental. Stripes, conventional in colour and old-fashioned in style – or so I thought at the time. But there was one that jumped out at me. It was – if I recall correctly – orange and red. Striking, in fact eye-catching. Without hesitation I took it.

Mummy smiled when she saw my choice. I assumed she was amused by the bright colours but as she said nothing we left it at that. The party began, I overcame my nerves and slowly, cautiously began enjoying myself. And then it happened. A tall, dark gentleman strode up and as I looked up at him I noticed he had on an identical tie.

'Young man,' he started, 'where did you get that tie?'

'Oh,' I replied, somewhat sheepish about the admission I was forced to make. 'From my father's cupboard.'

'And do you know that you're not entitled to wear it?'

'Why?' By then my voice was barely a whisper.

'Because it's the Colonel of the Guards' tie. Your father held the post and so do I but I don't believe you do.'

Perhaps he was teasing but I never wore it again. I never had the guts to risk a repeat. In the meantime regimental ties came back into fashion and London stores were overflowing with them. I often thought of buying one but memories of the last time I had worn one would flood back and I would walk away. If only I were 'entitled' to wear one.

Last Sunday that happened. I was invited by General Rai to speak to the Rajputana Rifles Officer's Association. The Raj. Rif. is Daddy's old regiment and I was visiting the officer's mess after almost forty years. As an unkempt civilian I must have stuck out like a sore thumb but I was nonetheless welcomed and presumably forgiven. When I left General Rai gave me a large wrapped present. I waited till I got into the car to open it. I assumed it would be a fancy calendar or perhaps a regimental insignia of some sort. I was wrong.

It was the Raj. Rif. tie. Deep green with bright red stripes. Dignified, distinguished, dashing. I've always wanted to wear it. Lewin's in Jermyn Street, one of my favourite shirt shops, has a Raj. Rif. tie hanging in the display window. Many are the times I've been tempted except memories of the Colonel of the Guards' came in the way. Now I had been given one by the Raj. Rif. officers themselves.

I'm not an officer and I doubt if I'm a gentleman but I do have a regimental tie with full authority to wear it. I'm itching for the next general to walk up and ask questions.

17 April 2000

Chapter 3

A Chip Off the Old Block

'If your teeth were as white as your hair you could advertise Colgate!'

Of Priests and Presidents

A.P.J. Abdul Kalam reminds me of the man who married me, if you know what I mean! He was a Catholic priest from Scotland. His name was Terry Gilfedder. Sadly, the last time we met was thirteen years ago. But I remember him clearly and the similarity is striking.

Last Saturday as I listened to the president I could hardly believe what I was hearing. He was addressing the boys of the Doon School. It was the 67th Founder's Day and Dr Kalam was the chief guest. But the subject of his speech took me back twenty years to December 1982. The same thoughts – in fact, the same phrases – were also spoken then. But that was no school function nor was I at the time a young boy. It was my marriage, Father Terry was the presiding priest and the words that came racing back to my mind, as I heard the president's speech, were from Father Terry's sermon.

President Kalam spoke of his recent visit to the Tawang Monastery. 'What advice can I take back for the people of India?' he asked the priests. Their answer was the subject of his Founder's Day address.

'Put aside violence,' they said. The priests are Mahayana Buddhists famous for their *tangkhas*. Forty years ago they gave my father one and it remains one of Mummy's prized possessions.

'And how can we do that?' the president asked.

'By sublimating ego. It's ego that is the core of selfishness and from it stems all violence.'

'But how can this be done?' the president persisted. 'How can we control our egos?'

It was the answer to this question that took me back twenty years. Back to my own age of innocence and incomprehension; when you listen but don't necessarily understand.

'Learn to forget the I and the Me.' That was the answer. Simple, stark and short. I don't know how many of the 440 boys or their parents and guardians understood. But when I heard the same words twenty years ago I know I did not. As I sat listening to the president, on the main field of the Doon School, my mind flashed back to a small church in Nottinghill Gate, just off Westbourne Grove, on a bright December afternoon. There Father Terry had said something similar.

'Karan and Nisha,' he said, pronouncing our names with the gentle lilt of his Scottish accent. 'I want to speak of three little words: I love you. Three words that symbolize today's ceremony and your relationship with each other. Love is the bond that unites you but if you forget that you are two separate people, with separate habits, wishes and rights, love will also separate you. Never forget that you are two individuals and never let the I in you overrule the you of the other.'

Isn't it strange that two men twenty years apart, one a Catholic priest and the other the president of India, should have found words so reminiscent of each other to express a thought so simple yet so difficult? Father Terry warned me against taking my wife for granted. President Kalam advised the boys of the Doon School against putting themselves first. But the point was the same. There is something beyond ourselves, as important if not more, and don't make yourself, your own ego, an obstacle reaching or understanding it.

I didn't heed Father Terry's wise counsel. To be honest, I did not fully understand him. Instead I laughed, as children often do, ridiculing what they cannot comprehend. I don't think the boys of the Doon School laughed. They are too polite, even too wise, for that. But perhaps they were bemused. When you are sixteen the I is everything. At their age, and for many years afterwards, my world was Me and I was the centre of it.

Today at forty-six I can see that other people matter because I have experienced how they do. That, I believe, is the catch. I learnt to see beyond myself when I discovered how it could help me. This means I learnt from my mistakes, from those dreadful knocks life deals each one of us, but that, sadly, is the only way one does. To be told is not enough. No priest and no president, no matter how sagely they advise or how seriously they warn, can make a difference.

Yet they are right to try. And do you know why? Because when your ego leads to your first fall and you start to nurse your bruises it's the sudden flash-like memory of their words – maybe long-forgotten but also starkly recalled – that helps you understand. It may be a lesson you don't heed but it's one you rarely forget. In need it usually comes back.

21 October 2002

A Calculated Affront

I've just returned from spending Founder's Day at Doon School. It was my first after nearly twenty-eight years. That's such a long time you actually don't remember what it used to be like. Instead, nostalgia and your own distorted memory create an impression that takes precedence over reality. But once back the old truths fall into place.

This year the chief guest was Arun Shourie and in his speech he complimented the school on its excellence. Arun was generous with his praise and justifiably so. As he spoke my mind flashed back to the Founder's Day of 1968 (or maybe it was 1969). Morarji Desai was the chief guest. He was also Indira Gandhi's deputy prime minister. Christopher Miller, the last Englishman to serve as headmaster, had invited him and the school was looking its best.

Desai arrived by helicopter touching down on the sacrosanct main field. He raced through the many interesting school exhibitions laid on for him. I was twelve and waiting to show him what I could do with pippettes in chemistry. But he was not interested. The photographs of the occasion show him looking over my tiny shoulders towards the exit.

It was Desai's speech that angered and hurt the school. To begin with he spoke in Hindi, a calculated affront to our English headmaster and a language he fully knew the boys could not easily follow. But Desai hated public schools and wanted to rub it in.

What I remember of his speech was the way he chided the boys for greeting him with a handshake. Why had we not done namaste instead? This, he admonished, was aping the West and forgetting our own culture. Indians, he said, sounding particularly supercilious, should always do namaste. The handshake was alien, improper and a characterless imitation.

It made us bristle. In those days politicians were not commonly disliked but Desai left school a universally hated man. He had barely spent two hours on the campus, claiming he had to get back in time to greet Mrs Gandhi on her return from a foreign visit. We were only too happy to be rid of him.

A surprise, however, was to follow. When the next day's papers arrived they carried front page photographs of Desai at the airport receiving Mrs Gandhi. And what was he doing? He was shaking her hand.

Desai had tried to belittle the school but in the process made himself seem small. Arun recognized the school's worth and visibly won us over. But I wonder if he noticed that it excels not just in the knowledge it teaches but, even more so, in the bigger, wider lessons it encourages each boy to imbibe. On the day he visited, the boys sang Song No. 3 from the school hymn book. It's by Iqbal, the man who first thought of Pakistan.

Lab pe aati hei dua banke
Tamanna meri,
Mere Allah burraie se
Bachanna mujhko.

As I joined in the singing, words long forgotten suddenly returning to memory in precise and perfect order, I recalled another truth about the school. At Doon you know nothing of caste or communal division. Ram or Krishna, Allah or Christ are the same. An Aggarwal and a Garg live side by side with a Rathore, a Vashisht, an Ahmed and a Henderson. And they all have silly nicknames.

23 October 2000

When Affection Is a Rude Joke

They say there's nothing more cruel than schoolboys. They're wrong. Far worse are those you were at school with – even after thirty years! My class of '71 at Doon had a reunion this weekend and I met up with several old friends I haven't seen for decades. But if anyone thought age, experience and wisdom would have curbed our penchant for laughter at someone else's expense – what I call digging it in – they couldn't have been more surprised.

'KT, just look at you!' was how I was greeted when I walked into the gathering. I soon discovered that the old school sobriquet was not used out of affection so much as to emphasize the comment that was to follow. 'If your teeth were as white as your hair you could advertise Colgate!'

Less obvious, though no less pointed, was the second greeting with which I was accosted a short while later. This time, however, I required the full recall of my literary memory to understand!

'Hey!' said a familiar voice not heard since the early 1970s. I swivelled in its direction to find a group beckoning me. They were clearly enjoying themselves. 'Do you think you're Mary's little lamb?'

'What?' I spluttered, perplexed by the simile.

'Well, its fleece was white as snow and so is yours!'

Fortunately, they tired of my hair fairly quickly. Unfortunately, that created the opening for jokes about my loquacity. To be honest, I don't think of myself as garrulous. But others do. Worse, my old school friends have also held firmly to the belief that I can't keep a secret. 'Telephone, telegram, tell Thapar' was the saying when we were fifteen. As far as this lot is concerned, it holds good even today.

After a series of comments such as 'who thought Tota would join the navy!' and '*Yaar*, I can't believe monkey's become such a hot shot,' attention turned to me. I knew I was in for another ribbing.

'KT, you chose the right profession.'

'Why?' I foolishly asked, falling into an obvious trap.

'Because you never let anyone talk in school. Now, as an anchor, you can keep on interrupting and claim you're doing your job!'

'In fact, why do you bother to have guests?' someone else butted in. He was smiling but his tone was pure stiletto. 'The poor chaps don't get a word in edgeways. Why don't you call it "Interview with Self"? You know you'd love that.'

To be honest I would have been disappointed – actually upset – if our conversations hadn't started this way. Schoolboy affection is always disguised behind barbs and innuendo. It's less obvious but far sturdier than what you later encounter. In fact, I would add that you can always rely on someone whose leg you can pull. But can you equally trust a man you are formal with? Humour dissolves more than differences – it eliminates reserve, eradicates pomposity and obliterates the need for silly white lies.

I'm not sure if day school students can meet up after three decades with similar camaraderie, but I suspect not. On the other hand, the gruelling experience of a boarding school – and, of course, our capacity to romanticize memories, forgetting the dreadful whilst exaggerating the comic and peculiar – ensures that a friendship is never forgotten. Whilst you may not meet for years – even decades – and that was true of many of the class of '71 – when you do you can strike a chord instantaneously. And even if the rekindled old flame may start to flicker and fade after a bit, it will certainly shine brightly for the duration of a reunion.

Wellington was only slightly incorrect when he claimed that the Battle of Waterloo was won on the playing fields of Eton. I suspect the roots of that victory more accurately stretch back to the pranks played in the dormitories, the punishments inflicted by prefects and the homework hastily completed with a little help from the class egghead minutes before submission. Such incidents may or may not have put iron in the Duke but, for the rest of us, they've promoted self-reliance, self-confidence and an ability to see the funny side of any predicament. What's more, they've forged bonds that have survived the test of time.

So even if schooldays are not the best in your life – and, actually, it would be rather sad if they were – the boarding school experience is undoubtedly special. But you have to know it to truly understand why.

26 October 2006

Amitabh, Naseer and Mummy

The last rays of the sun were just starting to disappear behind the deodar trees as the play began. It was twilight and there was a distinct nip in the air. But there was enough light left to notice the apprehensiveness of the couple to my left. I was in the Rose Bowl at the Doon School and the play was an English translation of *Charandas Chor*. Their son, Imad, had a small part. There must have been several other parents feeling equally tense. Thirty years ago mine too would have had to grapple with similar emotions. But the pair beside me were a little special. They were Ratna and Naseeruddin Shah.

'Poor chap,' I said, trying to make my voice soothing and my manner reassuring. 'Imad must be quite intimidated by your presence.'

'Not at all,' Naseer laughed. 'I'm the one who's quivering and shaking!'

The play began slowly. That's not the sort of comment any of the watching parents would have made. In fact if mine, way back in 1970, had said something like that I would have been mortally offended. Parents are meant to encourage and applaud. But I wasn't there as a parent, only as an old boy. And this was the first time I was sitting in the audience watching a school play. On previous occasions I had been part of the cast.

Yet from the outset the mood of anticipation was clearly palpable. Everyone seemed to be anxiously waiting. The pace of the performance hardly mattered because the sense of expectation was so strong. But what was it, I asked myself, they were so keyed-up about? It reminded me of the audience at a production of *The Little Foxes* in London in 1984. On that occasion everyone was sitting forward, craning their necks and struggling for a better view. Then the explanation was simple. Elizabeth Taylor was playing the lead role. Here, at the Doon School, the answer eluded me until Naseer gave it away.

'There he is,' he suddenly whispered into my ear. 'In the *dhoti* entering from the left. That's our son.'

When you have a son on stage you don't need Elizabeth Taylor to excite you. The only difference was that the audience in London greeted Taylor's performance with loud oohs and ahs. At the Rose Bowl, the parents responded to their children with nervous little laughs followed, of course, with broad happy smiles. I'm afraid I watched as much of Naseer and Ratna – albeit from the discreet corner of my eye – as I did of their son.

Charandas Chor took me back thirty-three years to April 1968. In the same Rose Bowl – practically on the same spot where last weekend Imad had stood – I recall the young Vikram Seth standing. In a captain's uniform with a false moustache to make him look manly, he was playing the Chocolate Cream Soldier in Shaw's *Arms and the Man*. He was the star of the show and I had only a small insignificant part. But I was his nemesis. Engaged to the daughter of the house, he gets caught flirting with the maid. That was me. In those days the boys of the Doon School, like early Roman actors, played all the parts in a play.

As Vikram embraced me I was supposed to fall into his arms. It was, after all, seduction. But as he held me in a clinch – or whatever was permitted of one – my stockings started to roll down. As his ardour grew stronger my legs slowly turned bare. By the time he had me in his grip I looked more comic than alluring.

'Pull up your stockings, *yaar*,' someone shouted from the stands. Your peers can be merciless when you are twelve.

'Forget about her, Vikram,' said another voice. 'She's got hairy legs!'

❃ ❃ ❃

This year the Founder's Day chief guest was Amitabh Bachchan. I believe I was the one who suggested his name but I could be wrong. Although there were some who thought otherwise I feel it was an inspired choice. In previous years the chief guests have been men of distinction: prime ministers, chief justices, prize-winning authors, even the Dalai Lama. Amitabh is equally distinguished but he is also something more. He is popular. He was chosen not to please the teachers or the parents but the boys.

Of that there can be little doubt. Long before he arrived the whole of Dehra Dun knew he was coming. An hour before his car drove into school the gates were shut to keep out the crowds. Inside, the Rose Bowl was crammed to capacity. There wasn't room to stand but there were still many who could not fit in. The overspill of several hundred were seated on chairs outside, unable to see him in person but with access to a large screen replay.

For the headmaster, who speaks first, it was a hard act to precede. Even the parents, who normally pay close attention to his annual report on the school's performance, were impatient to hear Amitabh. And the chairman of the board of governors, who was next, knew he was only getting in the way.

So when Amitabh got up to speak he was heard in pin drop silence. I don't remember any shuffling of feet or crossing of legs. I don't recall hearing a single cough. And, yes, even the mobile phones seemed to go silent.

His rich deep baritone filled the Rose Bowl. In response, a sea of smiling faces looked back at him. I'm sure many did not pay attention to what he was saying. It was the power and impact of his delivery that mattered or just the fact that he was there and speaking to them.

I tried to listen and there was a lot I liked about his speech. But unless I misheard him there was one moment when I wondered if he really meant what he was saying.

'Schooldays are the best days of your life,' he said, repeating the old cliché most boarding school students distrust. 'Cherish them and believe me when I say things get worse after this.'

He may be right but isn't that a depressing message for teenagers to hear?

❁ ❁ ❁

If AB was in the limelight on Founder's Day the next belonged to his friend, Amar Singh. He came with Amitabh Bachchan but the school talked about him long after Mr Bachchan had left. The reason was that to everyone's astonishment – and to many people's delight – he gave the school a donation of ten lakhs. I'm not sure when something similar last happened. Unsolicited gifts are what the board dreams of but only rarely do they materialize.

Of course, there are those who question Mr Singh's motives but I think they are being unkind. It doesn't matter why a man gives money – whether it gives him happiness or publicity. What counts is that those who need it should receive assistance. Today if an additional boy can be given a full scholarship to the Doon School that's money well spent.

To his critics the Amar Singh scholarship may be an oxymoron but to the beneficiary it can only be a boon.

❁ ❁ ❁

Sunday nights after Founder's Day are depressing. Each year a pall of gloom descends over the Doon School. The festivities are over, your parents have gone and all that is left is the prospect of Monday morning school. I used to think of them as one of the worst nights of term and I can't believe the boys don't feel the same today.

In fact, what makes matters worse is that your parents always leave affecting an air of cheerfulness. My mother would depart smiling. I'd be close to tears but there wasn't even a hint of emotion in her voice. I used to think she was happy because she was leaving me behind.

This year, however, I saw Sunday night from the other side. On a train full of returning parents I realized how hard the wrench can be for them. It was their mobile phones that gave the secret away.

Normally I disapprove of people who make pointless conversation on trains or planes. They have nothing to say but nonetheless say it ostentatiously. But last Sunday the conversations were a revelation.

'Hello, *beta*,' I suddenly heard a voice say out loud. I turned to find my neighbour speaking. From the chord leading to his earpiece I concluded he was talking into his phone. His face was sombre. His eyes were moist. His voice sounded heavy.

'So, son, three days are over and another Founder's Day is done. It was good to see you, *beta*.'

I couldn't hear what the son said but after a while the father spoke again.

'*Hum* Saharanpur *pahunch gaye hein aur phir kuch ghantoon mein Dilli. Ab chutthi khattam aur kal office jana hei. Achcha nahin lag raha.*'

So does that also mean Mummy's big smile and cheerful voice were put on?

22 October 2001

Chapter 4

A Bit of a Brown Saheb

'A bit of a brown saheb, eh?'

Lessons from the Underground

Its official name is the London Underground but everyone calls it the tube because that's what it looks like. But actually, when you see one of the trains emerge out of a tunnel and approach the platform, I'd say a comparison to toothpaste would be more apt! Anyway, that's what I thought when I saw my first tube at the age of sixteen. I was at Victoria station, having just disembarked from the airport coach, with two enormous boxes on either side. Believe it or not, but the Air India flight from Delhi was two hours early and Kiran, my sister, with whom I had come to stay, was taken completely by surprise.

'Take the coach from Heathrow and then the tube to Bond Street' were her crisp instructions once she'd recovered from the shock of a brother arriving for a holiday ahead of time. 'I'll be at the other end.'

Bond Street was around the corner from Kiran's office but for me, new to London and both excited and anxious, it was a name from Monopoly. The mass of people was startling. They all seemed in a hurry but also very businesslike. Whilst the few who were lounging around, with spiky hair and broad bell-bottoms, appeared disconcertingly mod. In my grey flannels and ill-fitting school blazer I knew I looked like the outsider I felt I was.

It was in the middle of this reverie that the train suddenly appeared. A rumble from the tunnel heralded its imminence. The others recognized the sound and prepared themselves for its arrival. Since I was new and unfamiliar I continued to stare at things uncomprehendingly.

'Cummon, mate,' someone shouted at me. The train doors had opened and people were rushing in. But I was grappling with my boxes. When I grabbed both I had no arms left for my hand luggage. And if I tried to tuck the smaller pieces under them I could no longer lift the boxes.

'You could certainly do with a hand,' the voice continued. 'Maybe even two or three!'

It belonged to a man I presumed to be in his fifties. He had on a cloth cap, looked unshaven and his clothes were unkempt. Perhaps he also smelt. Ordinarily I would not have spoken to him. In fact, in later years, I would deliberately move away from others who resembled his type. I thought of them as tramps and would observe them from a distance out of the corner of my eye. My distaste would have been obvious.

But on this June morning things were different. I was young, in need of help and not yet a snob. More importantly, the man had grabbed my boxes – and some of my hand luggage too – and hauled them onto the tube. As the doors shut behind us, he turned and smiled. His teeth were stained and several were missing.

'Did it!' he exclaimed.

I wasn't sure what to say, so I smiled weakly.

'But it was a close thing.'

I was gauche and still scared of strangers. He was unused to making small talk. So we travelled in silence. But after the second stop he looked at me and asked, 'Where to, mate?'

He heard my answer with a nod before turning to look out of the window. All you can see from a tube are the black walls of the tunnel but he stared at them with mesmeric fascination.

I was dreading the end of the journey. How would I get my

luggage off? But when the train approached Bond Street I found the man had picked up the boxes before I could.

'You take the smaller stuff,' he chortled. 'More your size!'

He escorted me to the end of the platform. 'There you are,' he said. 'Good luck.'

Then he doubled back to wait for the next tube heading in the same direction. We never met again and I don't think I thanked him properly. But for me he has become an example of the sort of happy encounter one can expect on the underground. Unknown people who perform unexpected kindnesses and then disappear from your life. Of course, the opposite can also happen but I choose to remember the first sort.

As the metro goes underground in Delhi, I'm sure you will soon have similar stories of your own. They prove that people are never what they seem. And, yes, that our first impressions can be very wrong.

23 December 2004

Words of Advice for the Silly Season

It's the silly season again. That's a British term for the time of year when politicians take off on holiday and television devotes itself to old movies and re-runs. The Indian equivalent is determined more by the absence of MPs than by the content of telly. But if you make political programmes – or watch them – it cannot have escaped your attention that most ministers have migrated to cooler climes. Well, good luck to them. I write not to criticize but to advise.

As London is their favourite port of call, how will they be perceived in the British capital? As visiting Indians, as wogs or as undesirable aliens? I lived there for over two decades and the answer depends on who is observing you as much as on what you are saying, doing or wearing whilst being observed. It's very much a two-way process.

Let me explain by example. The first is from as far back as 1973. I was seventeen, still in school, uncertain, unsure and innocent. I was part of a school party that had gone to Stratford to see Coriolanus. However, Shakespeare wasn't the attraction so much as the chance to escape from Stowe.

During the interval there was – as there always is – an enormous rush at the bar. Everyone was queueing for a drink. Not having the guts to imbibe in public, I was in line for an ice-cream. As we slowly shuffled forward I started talking to the man in front of me. We were near the end when he suddenly asked:

'How long have you been in this country?'

'Just under a year.' In those days I still kept track of such things.

The first anniversary of my arrival in England was an event I was eagerly awaiting.

'Hmmm,' he continued. 'You speak remarkably good English. How come?'

'Because it's the only language I know!'

'Oh,' he replied. 'A bit of a brown saheb, eh?'

He meant no insult but he had unwittingly put his finger on the truth of my situation. The Jamaican community in Britain has a more colourful phrase for such people. They call them coconuts – brown outside but white within. I am not sure how many of our ministers would qualify as coconuts but I daresay many of them would be happy to be mistaken for one.

When I first arrived in England, the popular idea of India was determined by Peter Sellers, the corner-shop Paki grocer and the smell of curry and rice. Within a decade, however, this characterization underwent a dramatic change. By the time of Operation Blue Star, things were starkly different. Spielberg's *Indiana Jones* was the hit film of the year and *Private Eye* borrowed from its posters to respond to the storming of the Golden Temple. Its cover had Indira Gandhi, whip in hand, riding a chariot, galloping towards Harmandir Sahib. The caption read: 'Indira Gandhi and the Temple of Doom.' Quite how thoroughly Indira Gandhi had captured the British imagination became apparent soon after.

It happened three weeks later when I was sheltering in a taxi because a ceaseless downpour had made walking home from the tube station impossible. In fact I was lucky to find an empty cruising cab and get to it before anyone else. There was relief written all over my face but not that of the cabbie. Taxi drivers hate short hops, particularly at rush hour, and this was only a journey down to the end of the road.

'Awful weather,' I said, trying to be charming.

'Too bloody true,' came the terse reply.

'Been like this all day,' I gamely continued. 'I can't stand the rain.'

The cabbie kept silent. I was only twenty-six and unused to such situations. I carried on trying to make conversation but it was all in vain. I babbled on and on but his silence only grew louder. Finally, when we pulled up outside my front door the driver turned around and asked:

'And where you from then?'

'India,' I replied. It always amazes me when people ask because I can't imagine where else I could come from.

'The land of Indira Gandhi,' the taxi driver replied, smiling as he took her name. 'Good woman. I approve of what she's done to the Sikhs. Feel like doing it myself too.'

To be honest, in all my years in England I did not experience much overt racism. In fact, I don't think the British are racist. But they are xenophobes. They don't like foreigners and when they jest that wogs start at Calais they very definitely mean it.

The British have pejorative nicknames for almost every nationality. The French are frogs, the Spanish wops, the Italians are dagos, the Germans huns or krauts, the Americans yankees and the Arabs, who are thought of as the most distasteful of all, are pronounced *eyrabs*. But lest you get the wrong impression, let me add that the English do not spare their own. The Welsh are boyos, the Irish paddys or micks and the Scots … well, the Scots don't count at all. Indians used to be wogs. Increasingly, however, they are now called Pakis.

Yet at the end of the day the British only care about two things: your accent and whether you know which knife and fork to reach for when you sit down to dinner. Sadly, I can't advise our holidaying ministers on their accents. It's too late for that and their pronunciation is anyway incorrigible. But when it comes to knives and forks there is a simple rule to follow. Start from the outside and work your way in. So if there are three forks and three knives, the set on the extreme left and right is for your aperitif, the next pair is for the main course and the third for a savoury, if there is one. Dessert spoons and forks are usually at the head of the table setting, butter knives on your side plate and the big spoon – the one that looks like a little *karchi* – is for the soup.

Two other things: burping is not a welcome response to a good meal and it's polite to listen attentively to other people rather than talk endlessly yourself.

19 June 2000

My Cambridge

The door was ajar. Was that an invitation to walk in or simply carelessness? Unsure, I knocked. A loud but distant voice responded. 'Come in.'

I entered a square room lined with bookshelves rising to the ceiling. The curtains were drawn and the lights were not bright. The rich smell of cigar smoke hung in the air. It was a comfortable, well-used room but it was empty.

'I'm in the bath.' It was the same voice. 'Sit down and amuse yourself. I'll join you shortly.'

That was how Michael Posner, the man who would become my tutor, introduced himself. I would learn more of his eccentric ways in the years to come but at this first encounter I was flummoxed. I had come to Pembroke for an interview. Although anxious, eager and excited, I was ready for almost anything – but not this.

At eighteen I wasn't sure what to do. I wanted to behave like an adult but the question I could not answer was what would that amount to? I reached for a book and stood by an upright old brass lamp glancing at its pages. I can't remember its name but it had something to do with the Indian economy.

'Ah, there you are.'

I turned to find Michael Posner bearing down on me. He was a large man but his smile was equally generous. He thumped my shoulder and more or less simultaneously pushed me into a large armchair. Then he sat down in another in front of me.

'What's that?'

Posner reached for the book I had just put down. He seemed to know it.

'Well, young man, you want to come up to Pembroke, do you?'

'Yes, Mr Posner.' What else could I have said? The answer should have been obvious.

'In that case, what can you tell me about the Indian economy?'

It was a trick. And I had created the opportunity by choosing that particular book. I wished I had instead picked up a magazine or a newspaper. Now I had to talk about a subject of which I was completely ignorant. Inwardly I panicked but outwardly I started to gabble. It was the only way of covering up. I must have spoken for three minutes or more.

'Hmmm.' The sound was enough to stop my flow. But Posner was staring at the documents in his hand. I guess they must have been part of my application form.

'Not knowing the subject doesn't seem to be a handicap for you!'

Ouch! But there was a hint of a smile and his eyes were gleaming. That was the first time I saw Posner embarrass and applaud with the same sentence. It was his trademark style.

Eight months later, my A-levels completed, I arrived at Pembroke. It was a dark sultry October evening and the heavy clouds threatened rain. Having installed myself in my room and unpacked, I headed for the common room. It turned out to be in the same building as Michael Posner's rooms. As I opened the door to enter I noticed a large figure at the top of the stairs heading down.

'Is that the expert on the Indian economy or have I got it wrong?'

I blushed. I had hoped Posner would have forgotten the gibberish I spouted at the interview. But not just his size, his memory was also elephantine.

'Whatever else you do, you should join the Union.'

And with that he walked through the door I had just entered, leaving in his wake the warm feeling of a pleasant greeting but also a small niggling doubt that I had been put in my place. What was the Union?

The very next morning I made a determined effort to find out. An hour later I was a member. And for the next three years my university career centred around its large red brick building hidden behind the old Round Church. Posner had done me a second favour. I can only assume he sensed my ability to talk outstripped my talent for analysis and nudged me in this direction.

I was elected to the standing committee at the end of my first term and became president of the Union in the penultimate one. I wore *kurta pyjamas*, *achkans*, *bundgalas* and Daddy's old Edwardian double-breasted dinner jacket. Its broad watered-silk lapels were much admired. It was fun but it wasn't always frivolous. It made me realize that politics could also be a grind. Yet I can honestly add I don't think I've enjoyed anything more.

Three months later I graduated with a 2:1, which is good but by no means distinguished. Michael Posner must have guessed this would happen when he heard me spouting on the Indian economy. I bet that's why he pushed me towards the Union. Today I'd say he gave me the right advice.

12 May 2005

Anyone for Tennis?

'What's so special about Wimbledon?' Aru had just walked into my office and caught me watching a repeat of last night's match. I thought his question was a dig but his curiosity was genuine.

However, when I started to explain I realized how difficult it is to describe Wimbledon. No doubt tennis is international and television has made it truly global. And, of course, more people watch this game than any other sport on the box. But Wimbledon is far more than the All England Lawn Tennis Championship.

Wimbledon is summer and sunshine – though, ironically, it often rains and the games are washed out – it's champagne and pimms, strawberries and cream, privilege and passion. It's also – as only the British can manage – both patrician and populist. The Duke of Kent is as much a fixture as the ball boys. Venerable tradition sits comfortably beside McEnroe-style tantrums. Curtseys are as common as Anna Kournikova's short skirts. Wimbledon, after all, is a slice of Britain – eccentricity, exaggerated propriety, snobbery, yobbishness and an unabashed delight in the good things of life.

But how was I to explain all of this to Aru? As I tried his eyes started to glaze over. At first he seemed intrigued. Then perplexed. Finally, simply bored. Though we in India are crazy about cricket, we haven't developed similar traditions or conventions. For us the game itself is all-important. In Britain tennis is a metaphor for a style of life. Wimbledon is its apogee.

So I gave up and chose instead to tell Aru about my first visit to the grass courts of SW17. Nisha, my banker wife, had clients at Coca Cola who had arranged a marquee just off Centre Court. We were one of thirty guests invited on opening day. I decided to look sporty. I wore a rather natty double-breast blazer with a paisely cravat and a pair of linen slacks. I thought I looked fetching.

Now it didn't take long to discover that unless you really care for the game, it's far more fun quaffing strawberries and cream and downing champagne than sitting in the royal box straining to see the other side which, believe me, is pretty far away. So whilst the others watched I guzzled. And if you deign to see the lesser players then you can wander through the higher number courts carrying your champagne with you. By the way, Court One is for the big names but as the number increases the quality of player declines.

I ended up at Court 15, slightly woozy but intent on watching an Ecuadorian beauty demolish a Kraut vixen. A handful of supporters made it seem like a battle of the continents. The German would grunt, groan and smash the ball. The Latin American was all touch, drop-shot and delicacy.

Suddenly a man resembling a retired colonel – puce, bow-tied, tweed-suited – walked up and oyed me. Confident I wasn't the object of his attention I ignored him. But he continued. With each attempt his voice took on an edge and his manner seemed less charming. Finally he could no longer contain himself and burst out.

'Waiter,' he bellowed. I turned around wondering who he was addressing, only to discover it was me.

'Yes, you', the 'colonel' confirmed. 'What happened to the champagne and strawberries we ordered? It's been over half an hour.'

'Sorry,' I said needlessly. 'I'm not the waiter.'

'Aren't you?' the 'colonel' responded, by no means apologetically.

'The other bloke was dressed just like you. I thought it was the company uniform.'

On the tube home I repeated the story to Nisha. I expected sympathy but she threw her head back and hooted with laughter.

'Do you know why he said that?' she asked as if she knew.

'Why?' I replied, perplexed she should but also offended she was explaining away my little incident.

'Because you're overdressed. Only waiters care so much for their appearance. Real gentlemen wouldn't give a fig. Remember that the next time you go to Wimbledon.'

I was dumbfounded. Fortunately Aru seemed to miss the point as well. In his view the better dressed a man, the better the man is likely to be. Clothes, he believes, make a difference.

'Ah,' he clucked. 'So Wimbledon's a shabby sort of place.'

'No, not quite.'

'Then the British haven't got good taste.'

'No, not that either'.

'In that case,' he concluded, the penny finally dropping, 'there was something wrong with your clothes!'

Now tell me, could I have disagreed?

24 June 2005

Chapter 5

The View from My Window

'*Arrey ji* problem *nahin, Pradhan Mantri hai!*'

The Cost of a Wedding

There are times when I lose respect for my countrymen altogether. One such is weddings – particularly the grotesque, garish sort that occur at rented farmhouses in Chattarpur and Vasant Kunj, and especially when they take place together on the same night. It's a sure-fire recipe for man-made hell.

Last week there were several nights when the stars ordained that the middle classes could wed without fear of mishap. And they did. Except the mishap befell the rest of us.

Driving down the Vasant Kunj road at 10.20 one night, I suddenly found myself caught in a traffic jam. It began innocently, as if the lights had changed to red and the traffic had tailed back. But then it grew. After ten minutes it stretched further than I could see. A quarter of an hour later the road on the other side was blocked as well.

That's when misfortune started to turn to bedlam. Scooters, jeeps, then cars and finally small lorries drove down the grass verge trying to sneak to the front. A few of them got there and successfully blocked the only limited escape route left open. So the jam which was till then crawling ground to a halt.

Then drivers of various vehicles got out, sauntered off and went missing. Thus a quarter of an hour later, when one of the chaotic lanes got a break, inevitably some driver or other was absconding and cars on either side tried furiously to fill the gap. As a result one more cross-stream of traffic, this time running counter to the main jam, started up.

By now we were at sixes and sevens with cars pointing in every direction but the right one. A feeling of helplessness descended and people started switching off their lights. A strange dark fell on the road and it seemed we were locked in for the night.

I can't say how long this impasse lasted but it would have been well over an hour. At no point did the confusion clear. It simply, imperceptibly inched forward until the cause of the trouble came into view.

It was, of course, a wedding. The guests had parked – or rather abandoned – their cars on the road. Thus one lane out of three was blocked. The oncoming traffic, which had jumped the middle divider and tried to shoot down on the wrong side, had blocked another. Logically that should have still left one lane free but the middle one was preoccupied with a thousand small accidents. All those cars that had pushed their noses out, trying to get past out of turn, had hit each other. The damage done, their drivers were quarrelling over questions of guilt and compensation.

It was bizarre except it was also infuriating. With traffic snarled up over three miles even those drivers with a way through had chosen to add to the confusion by ventilating their spleen on another for a fault that was as much their own.

When, finally, I made it to the Vasant Vihar turning – what the authorities insist on calling Nelson Mandela Marg; poor chap, couldn't they have found a more salubrious road to name after him? – I was stopped by a posse of roadside policemen. They were, incidentally, the first I had seen that night.

'*Aap bhi* traffic *jam se aa rahen hein*?' they jocularly asked.

'*Ji haan.*'

'*Kitni der phasse rahe?*'

'*Ghante se oopar.*'

'*Achcha hua ki hum nahin gaye. Nahin to hum bhi us* problem *mein phass jaate. Khulne do aur phir hum pahunch jayenge.*'

Heaven protect us if the seven-lane national highway ever gets constructed. They're bound to build *baraatkhanas* on either side of it. That would be a traffic jam from Kashmir to Kanya Kumari, this time with the traffic police caught inside.

25 January 1999

Is the PM Listening?

I think it's time someone warned the prime minister. Though we love him dearly and care deeply for his security, there are limits beyond which it would not be wise to push this affection and concern. Holding up traffic – actually, bringing it to a complete gridlock – for an hour or more at a time, and often on two or three occasions a day, is taxing our endurance unbearably. It's pushing the good, patient but now also tired people of Delhi to the end of their tether. In fact, matters have reached a point where many have come to feel that if this prime minister's safety routinely and repeatedly requires the devastation of our lives then, perhaps, we need another. After all, he's supposed to be popularly chosen. Surely he can't be so unsafe in the midst of the very people who have voted for him?

I accept that these thoughts may seem uncharitable on a calm Sunday morning. After a good night's rest and a strong cup of coffee many might forget or even forgive the nuisance of the prime minister's convoy. And I don't want to resurrect the past week's traumas. Yet you only have to be caught in its wake once, sitting and fuming in your car, watching the bedlam grow around you, for your anger to seethe. At such moments the human kettle boils furiously and as it steams one's thoughts can turn feverish.

I recall returning to Delhi from Noida late in January. It was midday and we crossed the toll bridge at a speed usually only achieved on a German autobahn. It was exhilarating. There was laughter in the air. But when we got to the other side and entered

Friends Colony, a wall of stationary traffic brought the car to a grinding halt. At first I wasn't sure what had happened. Maybe there had been an accident? Perhaps a lorry had overturned? But as the minutes ticked by it slowly dawned that the problem was more serious.

'*Bhai saheb*,' I asked, lowering the window and addressing a pedestrian. 'Problem *kya hai*?'

'*Arreji* problem *nahin, Pradhan Mantri hai*!' and he laughed as he walked on. At least he was moving. I was confined inside a stalled car. There were hundreds behind whilst ahead the queue stretched over the bridge, past Lajpat Nagar and beyond as far as the eye could see, perhaps all the way to South Extension. A four-mile tailback and we were at the far end of it!

It transpired the prime minister had an appointment in Nehru Place. From where I sat his destination couldn't have been farther away. Yet roads in every direction had been sanitized, sealed and shut. He stayed barely five minutes. We were locked in traffic for fifty-five.

My colleague Ashok, who was travelling with me, was philosophical to begin with. '*Yeh hai* democracy Indian-style,' he said with a smile.

Ashok is a placid personality. His fuse burns slowly. But before long the wait got to him. Slowly but steadily his comments acquired an acerbic character.

'*Inko* helicopter *se jana chahiye*,' he commented, staring despondently into the river of traffic ahead. '*Ya ghar pe rehena chahiye*,' he added ten minutes later. This time his voice was less audible. He sounded in despair. '*Yeh log harenge*! *Dilli me burri tarah harenge*,' he suddenly exclaimed at the end of half an hour. Except now he was also smiling. His eyes were lit up. I guessed it was the sweet thought of revenge.

Of course, it doesn't have to be like this. Last week, in

Washington, I was one of 3,500 guests who breakfasted with Bush without inconvenience or needless delay. No doubt we had to walk through scanners and each of us was frisked. But it was fast, efficient and orderly. No one complained. Outside the Hilton Hotel traffic flowed normally. Yet inside the president was safe and his security satisfied.

Almost twenty years ago, the week after the Brighton bomb that nearly killed her, I was standing outside the House of Commons as Mrs Thatcher drove out. It was peak time. The rush was heavy. But traffic was stopped for barely ten seconds before her car emerged from the gate. Immediately thereafter it resumed. There was no lengthy convoy, no ambulances, no accompanying police jeeps. Yet Mrs Thatcher had just brushed with death and the IRA were as vicious as our Kashmiri brethren today.

So my advice is short and simple. Mr Vajpayee should change his security, use a helicopter or stay at home. And I'm not being facetious. If it's difficult for the PM to cross the city let its citizens come to him. I'm sure they'd be happy to – and that would make the rest of us happy too.

17 February 2003

One Invitation Too Few

Come December and I start to dream of long cold nights, a blazing log fire, something hot to drink and someone to warm the cockles of my heart. After all, that's what winter is supposed to be all about.

Not in Delhi. In our city winter is a mad whirligig of cocktails, receptions, dinners, weddings, frenetic socializing and ceaseless social climbing. If you're not invited to one of each your popularity has sunk. If you attend all of them you're a star.

What counts is not the fact but the perception. Image is all, as I discovered to my cost. Last week I was invited to dinner. The invitation said 8.30. Knowing my hostess was Indian I opted to be an hour late. Unfortunately, I was still too early.

'Oh, fancy you turning up so early,' she greeted me as I stepped into her bare drawing room. 'Didn't you have anywhere else to go tonight?'

I don't think she meant offence. She was simply surprised I had arrived by 9.30. No one else was expected much before 10.00 – including her husband. In fact, most of the guests turned up even later – that is to say those who bothered to come at all. All of them had other parties to attend first. Some got stuck en route.

Which suggests that to be the recipient of just one invitation can be uniquely problematic. You are probably the only one in that position, leaving you with the horrible conundrum of when to turn up. Whenever you do it's not likely to be convenient. If you're too early your hostess will probably feel she's invited a reject. If you're too late you at least will feel guilty about your unpunctuality. It's probably safest not to go at all.

My own problem is even worse. It's compounded by the fact that there is another Karan Thapar. As if one wasn't bad enough, two of us makes for almighty confusion.

On the 29th of November *he* hosted a polo match. Except the press mistook *him* for *me*. So if there's any kudos in spending a few crores on ponies, smart pants and pretty fillies *I* got it and not *him*. To make matters worse one newspaper actually had the gall to ask why *he* was wasting time on election day watching polo when *he* could have been analysing the election results. Poor devil and what a waste of the family's dwindling fortune.

Then last week fate took its revenge. It was my turn to be at the wrong end of the confusion of identities. Someone rang my secretary to ask why I had not responded to a much sought-after dinner invitation for the 10th.

'Because he hasn't received the invitation,' the indomitable Aru replied with an aplomb that would do Jeeves proud.

'We sent it to Safdarjung Enclave and the courier receipt says Prem Bahadur received it.'

'Ah,' said Aru, this time more like Sherlock Holmes. 'But Mr Thapar doesn't live there and there's no one called Prem Bahadur that he knows. I think you want the other one.'

They did. He went to dinner. I spent my first night by the log fire – or at least I would have if for once I had not received two other invitations for the same evening!

9 December 1998

Chapter 6

The Little Things that Matter

'Now that you've rung let's have a chat.'

Reply and Revenge

Do phone calls from banks offering loans or credit card companies flogging their products irritate you? Do you find that your temper flares and you rudely cut them off? But then, your anger spent, do you have moments of remorse when you feel you should have handled the matter less wrathfully? With more restraint and less fury? Finally, do you end up annoyed with yourself? Promising that next time, though firm, you'll also be more polite?

Well, that's exactly how I would react each time my mobile rang and I answered an unsolicited enquiry. It could happen up to five or six times a day. Sometimes three times an hour. Even whilst I was away in London or Singapore!

But no more. I've found a solution that not only takes care of my petulance and anger but, more importantly, is a powerful antidote to the persistent callers. It's the perfect remedy. It's simple, effective and yet completely reverses the tables. I find it delightful. Irresistible. And most enjoyable.

The trick is to engage the calling party in a prolonged and polite conversation. They've called to ask you questions but if, instead, you start putting the queries and do so with the same enthusiastic curiosity they deploy, it really stumps them. It also gets their goat. Before long they will bang the phone down. And you'll be left laughing.

Let me illustrate with an example from yesterday.

'Is that Mr Thapar?' It was a female voice and sounded well-practised.

'It is indeed, my dear,' I replied. 'How very good of you to call. What's your name?'

'Monica.' But she sounded somewhat surprised at my friendliness.

'Monica,' I responded, as if I had been waiting for her call. 'What a lovely name. How are you? And where did you get my number from?'

Monica wasn't sure what to say. Or, at any rate, if she said anything I couldn't tell what it was. But she did mention she was from the ICICI Bank.

'Never mind,' I continued. 'Now that you've rung let's have a chat. Tell me about yourself. How old are you?'

'Why do you ask, Sir?' This time Monica sounded a little worried.

'Oh, purely out of curiosity. But I realize it's rude to ask a girl her age. So tell me, where do you live?'

'Why?' Now her voice sounded very short, even abrasive.

'Just like that, but don't worry. Maybe you would prefer to tell me where you went to school and what your favourite subject was?'

At this point Monica disconnected. As far as the ICICI Bank is concerned, it was a wasted phone call.

An alternative version of this tactic is the one I tried on a caller who said he was from American Express. It happened a few days earlier.

'Good morning, Mr Thapar,' said a male voice sounding rather pleased with itself. 'My name is Varinder.'

'No,' I responded, 'you're joking. You're not Varinder. You can't fool me with that one.'

'I am, Sir'. The poor chap responded, quite flummoxed by my refusal to believe him. 'I promise you I am.'

'But you sound like a Vinod, not a Varinder. Or maybe possibly a Vikram. Varinders have much deeper voices.'

'Sir, I am Varinder from American Express. I promise.'

'Funny,' I said. 'I once knew a Varun at Amex. Do you know him? Tall chap with a nice smile. Perhaps thirty years old.'

'No, Sir,' replied Varinder, wondering what was happening.

'Well if you ever meet him do say hello. I hope he remembers me.'

'I will, Sir.' And then Varinder hung up.

I accept you could say this is just playing silly games. It is, but so what? What makes such tactics such fun is that they take the mickey. What they do is lead those well-trained telephone voices, who have been taught to be unctuously polite and sugary sweet, into losing their cool. Slowly, steadily but surely they fall into a well-laid trap. Not for a moment do they realize what's happening until it's too late. And when, finally, it dawns on them, they've already been done for.

It's cold-blooded calculated revenge. And I recommend it. No doubt the phone calls will continue but your resentment of them and your anger at yourself for not handling them with greater poise and thoughtfulness will cease. In fact, for a while you will eagerly await the next one.

So ring away ICICI or Amex, HDFC or Hutch. I'm waiting for you!

9 February 2006

The Truth about Cricket

It was 7 in the evening and the end of a long and tiring day when she rang. Some of you may think that accounts for the answer I gave her. A few might even feel I was trying to be funny. But the fact of the matter – if you're ready to believe it – is that I was speaking the truth.

'What do you think of cricket?' she asked. From her voice I could guess she was one of those pretty young things who masquerade as journalists. In fact, that might also have had an impact on my answer. First impressions, after all, can be telling.

'I don't think about cricket,' I replied, stressing the second word. I was trying to be both witty and succinct. But she only giggled. Sweetly, no doubt, but disconcertingly nonetheless.

'Tell me something more,' she said flirtatiously, after recovering her composure.

'Why?' But I was only half teasing. The other half was intended as a challenge.

'Because I want to publish your answer and the first won't do!'

I suppose her bluntness got to me. But she also had a point. What would I do if those I professionally question chose to answer as I did? At any rate, whether out of sympathy or vanity, I found myself tempted to speak. I should have resisted because once I began I was caught in a trap. As the conversation developed I found myself sinking.

'I find cricket mindless, dreary and tedious,' I said. I tried to sound tongue in cheek but the truth is I was saying what I actually feel. I don't like the game. I don't even understand it. And when I find myself forced to watch I struggle to keep awake or, at any rate, sit still.

'How funny,' the voice on the other side of the phone commented. She wasn't giggling this time. In fact she sounded deadly serious. 'Why?'

'Because cricket is a game where eleven oafs in flannel chase a ball hit alternately by two others whilst a stadium full of duffers cheers them on.'

I'm not sure if I was consciously quoting but the mellifluous fluency of this pithy description did not sound original to my ears. Nevertheless, I was pleased with it. Not so the lady journalist.

'Oafs?' she queried. It wasn't the pronunciation she was uncertain of so much as the meaning. It transpired that she had mistaken it for a sylvan term. From little acorns do big oafs grow, if you catch my drift.

'Flannel?' she asked, once her first question had been taken care of.

'It's spelt ...' but she interrupted before I could finish.

'Like those people in a TV studio sitting together?'

This was my turn to laugh and I did so loudly.

'No doubt they're oafs too but I wasn't speaking about them.' I spluttered when I stopped guffawing. 'No, it's not television panel discussions I'm referring to but the clothes cricketers wear. White flannels.'

'But which is the team in white?' she asked missing, or at any rate sidestepping, my point. 'I thought everyone wore colours.'

'Of course they do.' But as I reassured her I realized the difficulty of extricating myself from a conversation that had not merely veered off course but perhaps entirely disappeared from the track. My heart sank and I opted for silence.

'Well?' she said after a bit. 'Which one?'

'None.'

'But you just spoke about oafs in flannel and you said flannel was white. So tell me, who is playing in white?'

'But that's not what I meant?'

'Then what did you mean?'

'Oh dear,' I exclaimed, somewhat exhausted by the prospect of putting matters right. 'I wish I knew.'

It wasn't a serious comment. In fact it was said more to myself than to her. But she pounced upon it with a journalistic ferocity that ordinarily I would have admired.

'Are you saying you don't know what you mean?'

'You could say *you* don't know what I mean,' I answered combatively. But she failed to grasp the twist in my reply.

'In other words you don't know what you're talking about?'

Perhaps she was right but I was stunned. In fact, quite speechless. The conversation had taken a bizarre turn.

'Yes, I suppose that's what it must look like.' My voice sounded defeated. In fact, clean bowled. 'But I did forewarn you, didn't I?'

'Well, I'm sorry I rang. I seem to have made a terrible mistake. Goodbye.'

I must have held on to the phone for a while – long after the line disconnected and a loud engaged tone started to emanate from the receiver – because when Aru walked into my office he thought I was in trouble.

'A problem?'

'Yes,' I replied. 'I just spoke the truth about cricket.'

24 February 2003

It's the Little Things that Always Matter

Have you ever done something silly and then worked yourself into a frightful tizzy about it? I do it all the time although that's no excuse or explanation. In fact it happened again last Tuesday.

I have this habit of washing my spectacles in hot running water each morning. I call it 'boiling-the-dirt' off them, although the procedure is neither as dramatic nor as effective as that would suggest. I simply hold them under a tap and then gingerly dry them off with soft tissue.

Now on Tuesday as I was repeating this daily exercise the little plastic nose-grips (Is that what they are called? That's certainly what they are.) fell off. Don't ask me how and please don't question why. I simply don't know. But it depressed and upset me no end.

If you look at a pair of spectacles – as opposed to wear them – the nose-grips are possibly the most irrelevant bit. Once the specs are on your face you can't even see them. But they are the little balancing devices that grip the bridge of your nose and prevent your glasses from falling off. So irrelevant though they may appear their function is vital.

The other thing is that my spectacles are new. I only bought them in January and I'm fond of them. They suit me, or so I believe and so I've been told. To have done an injury to their vital little bits just three months into their existence made the pain hurt all the more.

All morning I was restless. No matter what the task I was

attending to, or who I was speaking to on the phone, the spectacles with the missing little bits stayed at the front of my attention. I just could not stop thinking about them.

At lunch, too disturbed to continue, I walked out of the office to find an optician. I first tried Greater Kailash. It's just nearby. But being Tuesday it was shut. I then tried Vasant Vihar. But the only shop I know was closed.

By now my agitation was mounting, my glasses were slipping off my nose and my mood was glum. Sensing my desperation my driver suggested I try South Extension. I don't know any optician there but I readily agreed.

We stopped outside a shop called Gem Opticians. With my heart beating furiously I stepped in. What would I do if the glasses could not be repaired? The morning's little accident had by now blown itself into a major tragedy.

I explained my problem to the shop attendant. He looked knowingly at the spectacles and then he looked quizzically at me.

'Did you try and adjust these yourself?'

'No.'

'But these little bits are made to last. They don't break or fall off unless you've done something to them.'

'Honestly I haven't. Not a thing.' I pleaded. 'But can you fix them?'

'I'll try, Sir.'

For the next five minutes I paced the shop anxiously. I tried to look at the display shelves. Designer spectacles of all varieties lay there. Would I have to choose one of these as my new pair? The thought frightened me. No doubt the alternatives were far nicer, more expensive and infinitely more durable than my own but I like my glasses and I felt right in them. If spectacles maketh the face then mine was framed by the pair now under repair. I prayed all would be well.

'There you are, Sir,' the attendant's voice announced as he broke into my reverie. 'Unless you do something silly they should not break again.'

'Thank you,' I stammered and stuttered. I was incoherent with happiness and relief. 'How much do I owe you?'

'Nothing, Sir. We never charge for repairs.'

'But these weren't bought from you!'

'Well, Sir,' the man smiled, 'in that case let's hope that you buy the next pair from us.'

There are two morals to be drawn from this story and I trust you haven't missed either of them. Don't let little things get the better of you and, secondly, there are definitely a few good people in this world. In fact, some of them are true gems.

Oh yes, and if you break your spectacles or need a new pair, can I recommend Gem Opticians in South Extension, Part I?

26 April 1999

Yes, Sir or No, Sirree!

I'm beginning to fear I may have lost my name. These days when I walk into an office only a few people shout out 'Hello, Karan'. Instead, what the majority says is 'Good morning, Sir' or, if they're being friendly and informal, 'Hi, Sir'. What's even worse is the look of polite deference on their faces. It clearly establishes that 'Hi, Sir' is not 'Hi, *Yaar.*'

The problem is I don't think of myself as 'Sir'. In my mind I remain 'Karan'. But that's not all. I also still think of myself as youthful, cheeky, unpredictable and a little irrepressible. However, the term 'Sir' appears to contradict all of that. It sounds more like a response to my all-too-visible white hair rather than my self-assumed effervescence. It ages me and, worse, sets me apart. 'Sir' is never one of us. 'Sir' is inevitably and irresistibly one of them. 'Sir' is an alien.

However, compared to what happens outside the office, to be called 'Sir' is only mildly off-putting. Far more galling is the term of address strangers use. When I stop the car and ask for directions, or walk into a shop, or even pause to buy a paan, they call me 'Uncle'. Now it's one thing when little toddlers use the word and quite another when it trips off the tongue of a strapping lad of twenty-five who looms over you. Of course, he means to be polite. Of that I have no doubt. But it leaves me feeling aged and sometimes a little decrepit.

Alas, my misery is not about to end. Indeed the saddest part is the realization that things can only get worse. Soon – far too soon, in fact – the day will come when the awesome suffix 'ji' will be added to the already far too deferential 'Sir' and 'Uncle'. I dread the moment I become 'Sirji' or 'Uncleji'.

I recall the first time it happened to my sister Premila. She had been shopping in Hauz Khas and returned a little shaken. At the time she was probably no more than fifty. That, by the way, is my age today.

'What's the matter?' I asked. I was just about twenty-five.

'They've started calling me Mataji!'

'So?' I questioned, unable or unwilling to understand what she meant. 'What's wrong with that?'

'Everything. For a start, I don't look like a "Mataji" and, secondly, I never want to look like one. So when strangers call me "Mataji" I wonder what's gone wrong!'

I think I smiled. Or maybe I stayed straight-faced. But what I do recall is that I dismissed her complaint with an airy and rather unsympathetic wave of my hand. I simply couldn't imagine that one day I might face a similar predicament. Today time has caught up with me – and how!

The other day my nephew Udayan dropped by with his son Arzaan. Normally he's an ebullient and outgoing child. He's five and full of fun. But on seeing me Arzaan instantly transformed into a shy and tongue-tied lamb. The more I called out to him the tighter he seemed to cling to his father.

'Come on, Arzaan,' Udayan broke in, trying hard to help me. 'Go to Nanoo.'

'Nanoo!' I spluttered.

'Yes, Karan Mamu. That's what you are. You're his Nanoo.'

I'm not sure if my face fell but I do know that my desire to dangle the child on my knee disappeared almost immediately. Arzaan, oblivious of the angst he had caused his great uncle, continued to cling to his father.

It's only in India that deference and politeness are taken so far they end up feeling like victimization. In London if you aren't up to calling your boss by his or her first name you might end up saying 'Mr This' or 'Mrs That'. But no one would say 'Sir'. And certainly not 'Madam'. Such terms of address stop with school.

Now I concede Americans call everyone 'Sir' but there's neither deference nor any hint of age associated with the way they do. Their tone takes care of that. If not, their accent certainly does!

In India, however, you just can't win. A week ago I made a determined effort to put a stop to being called 'Sir'.

'Listen,' I said to someone who had been dropping the word like confetti. 'Won't you call me Karan instead?'

'Of course, Karan Sir,' came the reply. Then, after a pause, he added, 'Or would you prefer Thapar Sir instead?'

14 September 2006

Chapter 7

Getting Your Knickers in a Twist

'Her Royal Highness the Duchess of Cornwall has asked me to invite you to a Dinner Party.'

What Should I Call You?

English is a fascinating language. That its spellings are not phonetic and its pronunciation idiosyncratic is well known. But what is less familiar is that the meaning of a word sometimes depends on the tone with which it's spoken. Even more surprising is the fact that how you address someone reflects more than just your respect for them. It can also convey your recognition of their marital status or the longevity of their husband. This is why the English language has very specific terms of address. Sadly, few people today understand them.

To start with, terms of address, like those of endearment, can be misleading. For instance, not every use of the word 'dear' is endearing. Depending on the tone, the phrase 'dear boy' can be weighed down with sarcasm or even grounded in disgust. You have to listen to the voice to make out what is meant. That's also true of the way someone chooses to address you.

I was eighteen when I discovered this. As a young freshman at Pembroke, the Cambridge tradition of addressing undergraduates as 'Sir' was both pleasing and perplexing. No one had ever called me 'Sir' before; nor was I aware that the word can be used without deference.

So imagine my surprise when I was caught walking across the college lawns and hollered at from the Porter's Lodge. I knew such trespass was forbidden but I did not anticipate the response it would elicit.

'Get off the fucking grass, Sir!' the porter shouted. Usually he was a kindly old man in a bowler and bow-tie. Such language would have seemed impossible of him. But the sight of a student on the grass was more than he could bear. His use of the term 'Sir' may have been obligatory but it wasn't respectful!

On the other hand, we, in India, are guilty of unnecessary respect. When Benazir Bhutto was here last December the press – and almost everyone who met her – insisted on calling her 'Mrs' Bhutto. No doubt the fact that she is a Bhutto justified the surname but the assumption that she is 'Mrs' because she is married was mistaken. 'Mrs Bhutto' could be her mother or grandmother or either of her brothers' widows. But not Benazir. She's either Miss Bhutto or Mrs Zardari.

I realize that the conundrum lies in the question of how you address a married woman who prefers to be known by her maiden name. It's one we face in India as well. For example, how do you address Priyanka Vadra when she is using her maiden name? The English language – or do I mean English convention, although I would argue they amount to the same thing? – has the answer. It's as simple as it's straightforward.

If a woman uses her maiden name she must always be addressed as 'Miss' but if she uses her husband's surname she becomes 'Mrs'. So my wife was both Miss Meneses and Mrs Thapar. But Nisha could never have been Mrs Meneses or Miss Thapar. The former might be her mother, the latter could have been her daughter, but neither could ever have been Nisha herself.

The only catch is that this terminology reflects marital status and is thought to be sexist. Why, critics argue, should the way you address a woman turn on whether she's married when this doesn't apply to a man? It was to get around this that the term 'Ms' was devised.

Unfortunately, it's not an entirely successful creation. Nisha, to use her example, could have been Miss Meneses but what would have been the point of trying to be Ms Thapar? The term 'Ms' only works if you're not married or you're using your husband's name.

Of course, the delightful differentiations made possible by the English language go further. How you address a woman can reflect whether she's divorced or widowed. Again it's an ingenious little distinction.

Mrs Husband's-name Surname is a married woman whose husband is well and kicking, regardless of whether that pleases her or not. But Mrs Christian-name Surname is either a widow or a divorcee. So whilst Daddy was alive Mummy would have been correctly addressed as Mrs Pran Nath Thapar but after his death the accurate form is Mrs Bimla Thapar. To use the wrong one is misleading to those who know what it implies.

Today we no longer care about such conventions and that's a shame. Perhaps on occasion it's sexist or revolves around the husband and the marriage, but it's also informative and it does prevent little embarrassments. For example, no matter how often she hears it, to Benazir the words 'Mrs Bhutto' would always suggest her mother. If you think about it, that's probably true of most women as well. And, if you know better, you would never dream of asking Mrs Bimla Thapar how her husband is.

Modern language may be politically correct but it's often careless and can lead to avoidable errors. But do we care?

16 January 2004

The English We Speak

Do you know what makes the English we speak so different to that spoken by the British? It's not simply our accent and pronunciation, nor our vocabulary, or even our grammar, including the absence of it. No doubt those are some of the distinctions but they don't get to the heart of the matter. The 'core' difference lies elsewhere.

It's the way we express ourselves. The British use the language idiomatically. We speak far more literally. We describe what we have to say, we search out specific adjectives that convey our meaning and perhaps this is why in the process we use too many and usually all of the superlative sort. The British, on the other hand, prefer to express themselves with metaphor and aphorism. Consequently their language is rich with idiom. Ours is almost devoid of them.

Here's an example of some British idioms that we may be aware of but rarely, if ever, use ourselves. Their charm lies in the colourful – if at times bizarre – images they evoke. They add to the fun of the spoken language but also occasionally to its melody and beauty.

First, an idiom from an earlier generation: 'Don't teach your grandmother how to suck eggs'. Quite simply, it's a way of stopping someone from teaching you what you already know. But it also conveys a certain 'superiority' of age or, at least, of rank. The person being addressed is placed in the grandchild category. He or she is admonished for presumptuousness. The magic, however, lies in the picture the phrase paints – an elderly white-haired lady, perhaps her hair in a bonnet, devouring a collection of eggs by labial extraction.

Equally powerful is the image evoked by the more modern idiom 'Don't get your knickers in a twist'. This phrase was a favourite in the '70s and '80s, particularly with young women. It's a way of telling someone not to work themselves into an uncalled for rage. But it also goes further. It mocks the wrath, rather than treat it seriously or sensitively. Just as the picture of a person wringing his or her undies in anger would be ludicrous so, too, is the display of misplaced, if not misbegotten, emotion this idiom targets.

In fact, colloquial British English has several similar idioms. 'Don't get into a stew', 'Stop frothing' and 'He's all knotted up' may have slightly or significantly different meanings but they convey the same image of a person who has allowed himself to get entangled, a prisoner of his or her own anger and frustration.

One of my favourite idioms is the expression 'You look like death warmed up'. This phrase speaks at two levels. The obvious is that it's a way of saying the person addressed looks extremely unwell. Less apparent is that it's a way of expressing concern without slobbering all over the individual. It's expressive without being intrusive, it reaches out yet retains a certain distance. And, for all these reasons, it's quintessentially British. They use it all the time.

Perhaps from these examples it's obvious, but in each case the use of idiom alludes to, rather than specifically spells out, the thought you wish to convey. And, more often than not, it does so with goodwill and charm rather than a blunt outspoken statement of fact. Consequently, when your speech is flavoured with idiom, you can be both discreet and understated yet also rich and powerful in what you say.

The interesting thing is when we speak in Hindi – or, for that matter, in any of our other Indian languages – we use idioms all the time. So why is our English different? The answer, I suspect, is that English remains a foreign language. No doubt we have Indianized it with our disregard for conventional schoolbook grammar and our liberal cross-fertilization with desi vocabulary. But even so it remains pidgin, although in this case, of course, our own.

What we haven't as yet learnt to do – or found the confidence for – is to play with the language. Even our most proficient English speakers break into Hindi, or Bengali or whatever Indian language they know, when they wish to colour or reinforce what they have said by recourse to idiom. It's the point at which they become bilingual. Unconsciously or deliberately they are then escaping from their own limitations in English. It shows that whilst we may be fluent in the language we don't as yet feel comfortable with it.

23 March 2006

Random Thoughts for 2009

I doubt if 2008 could have been worse than it was. But now the most important question I can think of is, Can we be sure the new year will be better? I doubt if anyone knows. More significantly, I fear the portents suggest it might not be. So, whilst we apprehensively wait to find out, here's a little insouciance to cheer you up.

My cousin Ranjit has put together a collection of witticisms that seem remarkably apt in the circumstances. 'Smile, it makes people wonder what you are thinking'; 'The light at the end of the tunnel may be an oncoming train'; 'If you can't convince them, confuse them' and 'The road to success ... is always under construction'. Here's one, in particular, for smokers: 'The cigarette does the smoking; you are just the sucker'. And another for those who are married: 'Marriage is one of the chief causes of divorce'.

If you fancy yourself as someone who can turn a pretty phrase, Lakshman, another cousin, has sent me a few quotations you could easily twist for your own use. For instance, if someone's cracked a poor joke try Mark Twain's comment on Germans: 'Their humour is no laughing matter'. And if you want to rile a Bihari or a Bengali you can always adapt Sydney Smith's attack on Yorkshire: 'Never ask a man if he comes from Yorkshire. If he does, he will tell you. If he does not, why humiliate him?' Finally, if your neighbour and his pooch have got to you there's always Edward Abbey's riposte: 'When a man's best friend is his dog, that dog has a problem.'

Of course, most of the time when someone pops an awkward

question you're left searching in vain for something clever to say. The silence that follows is hideously embarrassing. Well, here are a few retorts worth remembering. Asked how many husbands she had had, Peggy Guggenheim replied: 'Mine or other people's?' Questioned by a rude TV anchor if she realized that the class system had ended, Barbara Cartland hit back: 'Of course I do, or I wouldn't be sitting here talking to you!' And then there's the old chestnut. When you're questioned about a disagreement with someone and need to explain it away, try this one-liner from the Cambridge Union: 'The difference between X and I is a question of mind over matter. I don't mind and X doesn't matter.'

Gen. Jacob, who's a bachelor, has sent me a collection of wisecracks about marriage. I wonder how many of you, joined in wedlock, agree with them? 'Two secrets to keep your marriage successful: first, whenever you're wrong, admit it; second, whenever you're right, shut up.' Here's another: 'The most effective way to remember your wife's birthday is to forget it once.' Yet one more: 'My wife and I were happy for twenty years. Then we met.' And finally: 'When a man steals your wife, there's no better revenge than to let him keep her.'

Meanwhile Bamby Rao has forwarded a list of what he calls 'gentle thoughts'. If the start of another year makes you feel conscious of how time is catching up, he's offering a little consolation: 'Eventually you will reach a point when you stop lying about your age and start bragging about it.' On the other hand, if you want to depress yourself, Bamby has another recipe: 'First you forget names, then you forget faces. Next you forget to pull up your zipper. It's worse when you forget to pull it down.'

And, do you remember Mary and the little lamb? Here's a version of the nursery rhyme created for that moment when Mummy is fed up of her little darlings: 'Mary had a little lamb, her father shot it dead. Now it goes to school with her, between two hunks of bread.'

Finally, if you love journalists as much as I do, be grateful to Humbert Wolfe: 'You cannot hope to bribe or twist, thank God, the British journalist. But seeing what the man will do unbribed, there's no occasion to!'

Happy New Year, or so I hope!

19 December 2008

Guess Who's Coming to Dinner?

We all play pranks but last month I was the target of a breathtaking practical joke. It wasn't simply sweeping in its scope but also meticulously researched and planned. Yet the amazing thing is I haven't the faintest idea who did it. He or she may have wanted to fool me – and might have partly succeeded – but shows no inclination of revealing his or her identity.

It began with the following email:

'Dear Mr Thapar,

Her Royal Highness the Duchess of Cornwall has asked me to invite you to a Dinner Party at Clarence House on 3 January 2008. Her Royal Highness and His Royal Highness The Prince of Wales are looking forward to having you with them. The Prime Minister and Foreign Secretary will also be dining with Their Royal Highnesses.

It is a black tie evening. If you would be so kind as to send me your address, I will post you an invitation card. You are expected at Clarence House at 19:15 hours, for drinks in the Blue Drawing Room. Their Royal Highnesses will receive you in the Imperial Room, where the Prime Minister will be joining their other guests. Dinner will be served at 20:00 hours.

I look forward to hearing from you.

Yours sincerely,

Robert Smedley-Smith, OBE,

Comptroller to The Household of Her Royal Highness The Duchess of Cornwall.'

The letter, I felt certain, was a prank. Clarence House doesn't use googlemail and such invitations aren't sent by email. But why was it copied to Richard Stagg, the British High Commissioner? The email given for him was correct.

I replied:

'Thank you for your letter of Saturday the 3rd of November. Forgive me for what might be a silly question but is this a joke? I don't believe that invitations from the Duchess of Cornwall are usually sent by email and that too from a googlemail ID. I may well be wrong – and if I am, I apologize – but I thought I should start by asking if this is a genuine letter or an elaborate hoax.

I'm marking a copy of my reply to Mr Stagg who, as it happens, knows me and perhaps he or you might send me a quick reply to confirm that this invitation is genuine.

As it so happens I'm likely to be in London on the 3rd of January and would be delighted to attend.

I await your reply.'

Within twenty-four hours I received two further letters. The first was from Richard Stagg. His simply said:

'Dear Karan,

I'm just off to London and will check (you may well hear in the meantime).

Best wishes,

Dickie.'

The other was from Smedley-Smith:

'I do apologise for the confusion. There have been some problems with the Royal Mail, which is why you have not received the invitation from Clarence House. Another invitation was dispatched on Friday by HM Diplomatic Bag to Dan Chugg at the British High Commission in New Delhi. You should receive it by Monday afternoon.'

This time the letter was not copied to the high commissioner.

But, I discovered, Dan Chugg does exist at the high commission. He's head of press. And the royal mail has been playing up. So, now, was the invitation genuine? I replied:

'Thank you for your letter. I also have a similar one from Richard Stagg who, in addition, tells me he's leaving for London and will double check and get back.

'I look forward to receiving the invitation you have sent by the Diplomatic Bag to Dan Chugg at the British High Commission.'

Three days later I received a phone call from the high commissioner's secretary. She had established that Robert Smedley-Smith didn't exist. The invitation – indeed the whole correspondence – was fraudulent. Someone had gone to great lengths to devise an incredible prank but refused to reveal their identity. And although I've waited for more letters they've suddenly stopped.

I doubt if I'll ever get a real invitation to dine with British royalty, but I wish I knew who to thank for this one or, at least, congratulate. Meanwhile, be warned if you receive similar letters. You could be the next victim!

26 November 2007

Thank God for E-Mail

I'm not sure what we did before the e-mail, but I doubt if reading unexpected letters was such fun. I have a collection of correspondents who often have me in splits. And I'm not talking of the ha-ha jokes, it's the funny peculiar variety I find most enjoyable.

For instance, last week my cousin Bharat Sahgal sent me the results of a first grade class test. Twenty-five students, each of whom is only six years old, were given half of a well-known proverb and asked to complete it. What they came up with is not just astonishing but rather clever and very funny.

Here are some of the results: Strike while the *bug is close*; Never underestimate the power of *termites*; No news is *impossible*; Don't bite the hand that *looks dirty*; A miss is as good as a *Mr*; The pen is mightier than the *pigs*; An idle mind is *the best way to relax*; Where there's smoke there's *pollution*; A penny saved is *not much*; Laugh and the whole world laughs with you, cry and *you have to blow your nose*; When the blind lead the blind *get out of the way*; If at first you don't succeed *get new batteries*; Two's company, three's *the Musketeers*; and, the winner, Better late than *Pregnant*!

Another gem was from Kris Srinivasan, a more regular source of e-mail wit and humour. But unlike Bharat, what he has sent are intriguing questions. You have to think of the answers as you read the following selection: 1) Why are a wise man and a wise guy opposites? 2) Why do overlook and oversee mean opposite things? 3) Why does no one say 'It's only a game', when their team is winning? 4) If love is blind, why is lingerie so popular? 5) Why is the man who invests all your money called a broker? 6) Do infants enjoy infancy as much as adults enjoy adultery? 7) If four out of five people suffer from diarrohea, does that mean the other one enjoys it? 8) If people from Poland are called Poles, why aren't people from Holland called Holes? 9) Why is it that people say they 'slept like a baby' when babies wake up every two hours? 10) If a deaf person has to go to court is it still called a hearing? 11) If electricity comes from electrons, does morality come from morons? 12) Why are you *in* a movie but *on* TV? However, my favourite is: If *I am* is the shortest sentence in the English language, could it be that *I do* is the longest sentence?

Of course, Kris's questions are capable of raising a few thought-provoking issues as well. For example, how important does a person have to be before they are considered assassinated instead of just murdered? To be honest, I'm not sure it simply turns on the victim's importance. Daniel Pearl was only a journalist but his death is spoken of as an assassination. The why and how of the murder could play a part as well.

But sometimes Kris can alarm you by the strange connections he is able to spot. Consider this: Do the Alphabet song and 'Twinkle Twinkle Little Star' have the same tune? Surprisingly, the answer is yes! If you don't believe me try singing the two songs and see for yourself.

However, when it comes to strange coincidences, Kartik Malhotra has stumbled upon the most bizarre. It seems the number 9 played an eerie role in Benazir Bhutto's life. She was born in 1953. That's 1+9+5+3=18 = 1+8 = 9. She died in 2007. That's 2+0+0+7 = 9. At the time she was 54. That's 5+4 = 9. But, hang on, Kartik isn't finished with just that.

The first suicide attack was on 18th October. The second fatal attack was on 27th December. And she was married on 18th December. Before that she was in self-exile for 9 years, starting in 1998 (1+9+9+8 = 27 = 2+7 = 9) and came back in 2007. Finally, written in Urdu, Benazir Bhutto has 9 alphabets.

10 April 2008

A Laugh for the New Year

Georges Clemenceau, France's famous World War I prime minister, once said of America that it was the only country in the world to have progressed from barbarism to decadence without experiencing the intervening stage of civilization. Perhaps he had American warning labels in mind. After reading about the US Wacky Warning Label Contest, now in its eleventh year, I decided to research the subject. What I discovered is both stupefying and hilarious. The Americans must be very special people indeed!

A label on a tractor reading 'Danger: Avoid Death' was adjudged this year's winner. Second prize went to another on a T-shirt that warns: 'Do not iron while wearing shirt'. A few years earlier the winner was a label on a baby stroller which proclaimed: 'Remove child before folding.'

The most striking conclusion about American labels is that they assume their countrymen are fools. Or how else do you interpret this caution on a bottle of drain cleaner: 'If you do not understand, or cannot read, all directions, cautions and warnings, do not use this product'? It's not by any means unique. Laser printer cartridges often state 'Do not eat toner', TV remote controls warn 'Not dish-washer safe', a toilet cleaning brush handle mentions 'Do not use orally', whilst a Halloween Batman costume advises 'This cape does not give the wearer the ability to fly'. Even hair colourings feel the need to add 'Do not use as an ice cream topping'.

Often the labels don't just appear to cater for the stupid or the utterly ignorant but perhaps also people who have abilities the rest of us cannot even conceive of. Otherwise why would a mattress warn 'Do not attempt to swallow'? Or earplug packages advise: 'These ear plugs are non-toxic but may interfere with breathing if caught in windpipe'? Perhaps Americans are zombies because hairdryers sold by Sears state 'Do not use while sleeping'. Or may be they are amphibious because some cars advise 'Do not drive in ocean'.

Or it's possible they're all sardars, and I write that with apologies to my twenty million brethren, Mr Badal and the SGPC. In my schooldays – long before 1984 – sardar jokes were the staple of schoolboy humour. What does a sardar milk bottle say at the bottom, we would ask? 'Open other end' was the answer. It may have been a dreadful PJ but, believe it or not, it appears to be true of America. My research on the net reveals that some Coke bottles in the US of A declare at the bottom 'Do not open here', muffins at a 7-11 store advise 'Remove wrapper, open mouth, insert muffin, eat', whilst espresso kettles helpfully advise 'This appliance is switched on by setting the on/off switch to the "on" position'. But surely the winner is this label on a microwave oven: 'Do. not use for drying pets'.

So does all of this mean Americans are a breed apart? Are they different or, at least, unique? Otherwise how do you explain these wacky labels? The truth is that Americans are no different to you and I, though a lot richer and occasionally not as cultured. Its their legal system – or their lawyers – that are to blame. Predatory legal-eagles file suits to claim damages for the most frivolous or far-fetched of reasons, thus forcing manufacturers to cover themselves by ensuring their products carry warnings advising against any conceivable misuse. And believe me I'm not exaggerating. You can even find bathtubs in New York which solemnly advise 'Do not throw the baby away with the water'!

But something else is also equally true. It's Americans themselves who have drawn the world's attention to these wacky labels and organized the wacky label contest. There's even a book on the subject. It's called *The 101 Stupidest, Silliest and Wackiest Warning Labels Ever*. So even in their lawyer-induced idiocy they retain their sense of humour. Frankly, that forgives a lot.

26 December 2007

Three Little Stories

It may be a commonplace thought but it's worthy of repetition. The politics of a country is defined by the character of its politicians. Which is why the opposite is also true: stories about politicians can reveal interesting insights into the political system they operate. And in case you haven't guessed, this is my excuse for telling you three little stories this Sunday morning!

The first concerns Harold Macmillan and the British election of 1959. At the time Super Mac, as he was called, was coasting to an easy victory. In fact, his slogan was the cheeky, if accurate, aphorism, 'You've never had it so good'. The country believed him. Which perhaps explains why his wife behaved as she did. She dozed off to sleep at the last Conservative Party political rally. Harold was speaking whilst Dorothy, for that was her name, was snoring.

'Oy,' shouted a man from the audience. 'Does His Bigness know that the Missus has dropped off?'

The remark brought the house down, leaving Harold somewhat abashed. But Dorothy, who had been roused from her slumber, wasn't the least bit flustered.

'My father is a politician, my brother is a politician, my husband is a politician and so are my son and son-in-law. I've heard what they have to say and I know it well. So, if you'll forgive me, I prefer to carry on sleeping.'

And she did but not before she had won the hearts of the audience. Harold, of course, won the election.

❋ ❋ ❋

The second story is about two of our own politicians. It was told to me at a recent dinner but, alas, I can't reveal by whom. However, its authenticity seems unimpeachable.

In 1984, after the assassination of Indira Gandhi, the shaken government struggled to arrange a suitable but secure funeral. Heads of state and government from all over were to attend and the arrangements had to be meticulous. The foreign office had reserved front row seats for each of them. But by the time Mrs Thatcher and Princess Anne, who were representing the British government and the British Queen, arrived, the row was full. Congress MPs, eager to be as close to the action as possible, had clambered over the back rows to occupy whatever empty places there were at the front. And so the two ladies remained standing whilst their anxious foreign office escort thought furiously about what to do next.

'It was a dreadful moment', my informant confided. 'The two ladies were definitely not happy but none of the wretched MPs would budge. They simply continued to sit there. Then, suddenly, a voice from in front of us rang out. 'Tell me, *yaar*,' it said, 'which of the two is more ugly?' And prompt came the reply: 'They both look like the backside of a DTC bus!'

❁ ❁ ❁

My final story comes from further afield. In fact, all the way from America, and it concerns the legendary FDR. It was told to me by Devendra Dwivedi, a politician of the old school with a fund of good-natured illuminating anecdotes. I need hardly add that Mr Dwivedi is quite unlike the two MPs referred to above.

One day at a meeting with a group of dissident senators, Roosevelt was berated for America's policy of support for an assortment of distasteful dictators. Batista of Cuba, more than any other, was the prime subject of concern.

'Mr President,' an overeager senator remonstrated. 'He's a son of a bitch.'

'I'm well aware of that,' the unflappable president replied. FDR was known for his sang-froid. But this was also a test of his political credentials, if not his integrity. 'But you know what? Batista is *my* son of a bitch. He's not *Stalin's* son of a bitch.'

American politics has always reflected the same cold, hard, self-calculating logic. Reagan and Bush may seem like excellent examples but I would argue that Carter and Clinton were no less, even if they found fine words to disguise it. Similarly, the Macmillan story captures a real truth about Britain. The British value humour. There's no lapse so terrible that a good joke cannot atone for it. And, finally, though regrettably, we in India are perfectly exemplified by the two MPs. I often grab seats meant for other people without any sense of remorse or shame. In fact I ignore the dirty looks I get. Our motto seems to be: take what you can before someone else does. And we do!

20 January 2005

In Praise of Repartee

I guess we live in a four-letter age. When we wish to retort or rebuke we tend to swear and curse. If we're English, speaking the F-word trips off our tongues with frightening fluency. The rest, I suspect, are prisoners of Punjabi invective. In either case, the crude, even the lewd, dominates our response. Sadly, we've bid goodbye to the use of wit and repartee.

How different was the world of Winston Churchill and Lady Astor. They seem to have been habitual sparring partners. Almost a century later, their stories are still delightful.

Once, when a tipsy Winston Churchill stumbled down the stairs of the House of Commons, he fell in front of a disapproving Lady Astor. 'Winston,' she reprimanded, 'you're drunk.' 'And you're ugly,' he shot back. Then, rising to this feet, he added: 'But tomorrow I'll be sober.'

At a dinner where Lady Astor was pouring coffee, she handed a cup to Winston Churchill with the words, 'If you were my husband, I'd poison your coffee.' Accepting, he replied, 'If you were my wife, I'd drink it.'

But it wasn't just Winston Churchill and Lady Astor who used their wit to keep the other in his or her place. Gladstone and Disraeli did the same in the nineteenth century. Gladstone, who was more proper and less flamboyant, was frequently at odds with Disraeli. 'Sir, you will either die on the gallows or of some unspeakable disease.' 'That depends, Sir,' Disraeli responded with a flourish, 'on whether I embrace your policies or your mistress.'

I suspect Disraeli usually got the better of their exchanges but Gladstone's description of him has achieved a certain rhetorical immortality. He called him 'a sophistical rhetorician inebriated by the exuberance of his own verbosity.'

The truth is that the English – and those who enjoy imitating them – delight in witty ways of putting the rapier in. They don't bludgeon but they delicately carve and slice. Consider the following put-downs. They make their point with great effect yet its difficult to be offended by them.

'He has all the virtues I dislike but none of the vices I admire' (Churchill); 'He has no enemies but is intensely disliked by his friends' (Wilde); 'He had delusions of adequacy' (Walter Kerr); 'A modest little person with much to be modest about' (Churchill); 'Some cause happiness wherever they go, others whenever they go' (Wilde); 'He uses statistics as a drunken man uses lamp posts … for support rather than illumination' (Andrew Lang); 'Why do you sit there looking like an envelope without an address on it?' (Mark Twain); 'He's not only dull, he's the cause of dullness in others' (Samuel Johnson); and 'In order to avoid being called a flirt she always yields easily' (Talleyrand).

It's not just authors or politicians who have a way with words. Occasionally, even Hollywood celebrities can be remarkably witty. Robert Redford once said of a fellow actor, 'He has the attention span of a lightening bolt.' And Mae West of a suitor who was less than ardent: 'His mother should have thrown him away and kept the stork.' My favourite, however, is Billy Wilder on an unkind music critic: 'He has Van Gogh's ear for music.'

In my time the Cambridge Union would applaud repartee far more than weighty and serious argument. The better debators always had a quiver full. The arrows were aimed at their opponents. A regular used to be: 'He's a well-balanced man with a chip on both shoulders.' Another was this comparison: 'The difference between Mr X and me is a question of mind over matter. I don't mind and he doesn't matter.' But the one that brought the House down was the Liberal leader Jeremy Thorpe's attack on Reginald Maudling, at the time a Conservative minister: 'They say when the going gets tough, the tough get going. Well, I suppose that explains why Reggie Maudling is sitting put in his chair.'

I'll always be a sucker for the deceptive charms of the good Reverend Spooner. Borrowing from his repertoire, I was once called 'a shining wit'. I beamed only to discover the quotation meant something very different.

10 July 2008

Chapter 8

Between the Covers

'And do you expect to be paid?'

Memory and Truth

An autobiography is a tricky thing. The problem is the writer is also the central character and usually ends up the hero. When that happens the book becomes an exercise in self-glorification – tedious for us though gratifying for the author. Which is why most Indians write dreadful autobiographies. They can't resist the temptation to blow their own trumpet. Everything they've done or said is always right; their opponents always wrong.

But I've just come across one that's different, though the reason is not simply a contradiction of the above assertion. Critics, of course, gleefully point to the author's tendency to omniscience. Maybe, but this book is special because it has interesting, even eye-opening, things to say. And it's readably written.

I'm referring to P.C. Alexander's *Through the Corridors of Power*. I chose it because I have a soft spot for the author. Way back in June 1984, days after Operation Blue Star, I flew to Delhi on behalf of London Weekend Television, searching for a minister who could be interviewed. Not conversant with Indian politicians, I had no idea how difficult this would be. As the shutters came down my request fell first on deaf ears and then on deaf phones. In desperation I turned to Swraj Paul in London. I knew he had contacts but I had no idea how good they were.

'Give me five minutes,' he said. 'Then ring P.C. Alexander.' From 5000 miles away this did not sound reassuring.

I rang and I can still hardly believe the sequence of events which followed. In an hour I was at Narasimha Rao's office. Thirty minutes later the interview was fixed. That evening it was recorded. By the 9th of June I was flying back to London, sipping chilled champagne as the plane carried me home.

So when I picked up his book I knew P.C. Alexander had been central to events in 1984. If anyone's account of Operation Blue Star mattered it had to be his. But what I had not anticipated was a critique of the army that would shatter all received wisdom. A week later I discovered Alexander's version is not uncontested. Lt Gen K.S. Brar, who commanded the Golden Temple operation, disputes almost every word he's written. Between the two the truth is hard to discern. Not being a historian I'm hardly the man for the job. But a debate has been opened and a controversy started. The unfinished analysis of 1984 has sprung back to life and is, again, a subject of discussion. For that we have to be grateful.

Alexander writes that Indira Gandhi originally asked for a siege of the Golden Temple to flush out Bhindranwale and the militants but Gen Vaidya, the then army chief, convinced her it wouldn't work and persuaded her to accept a commando operation instead. He assured her he could guarantee the safety of the buildings. However, Alexander points out, the general did not know the odds he would face. His intelligence was poor and his confidence misplaced. So when things went wrong the army – and, in particular, its chief – was to blame.

Baloney, retorts Brar, a siege was never possible. It could have lasted for months and *jathas* of aggrieved Sikhs would have converged on the temple. Punjab would have gone up in flames. As for the intelligence, it was never in the army's hands. RAW and IB controlled its source and carry the blame if it was faulty or misleading.

Alexander, however, goes further. He says the army rushed the operation. The generals could have taken their time but did not. So if lack of preparation added to the problem they have only themselves to blame.

Once again, Brar rubbishes this argument. Speed, he says, was of the essence because the militants were planning to declare Khalistan. The operation to oust them had to be completed before this happened.

Alexander also claims Vaidya failed to anticipate the shock Sikh soldiers would suffer. Consequently he did not prepare for this. However, nothing makes Brar more incandescent than this allegation. Being a Sikh he understands the sentiments involved but there wasn't much the army could do without giving the game away. Anyway, not a single Sikh officer rebelled.

No doubt, there's more to this dispute – both details and argument – and frankly I'm delighted. A chapter of our recent history previously put to sleep has been re-awakened. Only from the confusion that must inevitably ensue will the 'truth' emerge. But it can't be far away.

23 September 2004

I'm Sorry, Madhu ...

I wish I hadn't agreed to do 'something' with her book and, more than that, I wish I hadn't got carried away and reminded Madhu Trehan. I thought it would be explosive. Unfortunately I was wrong yet I still need to honour my commitment. That's my excuse and apology but will Madhu forgive me?

Madhu's book is about the Tehelka episode which caused a political earthquake in 2001. Any work that revisits the subject, with access to all the tapes and transcripts, including many we never saw or read, and interviews with the key players, should at least have caused tremors. Madhu suggested it would be a bomb. From what I can tell – and I must admit I can't bring myself to read all or even most of it – it's more like a dud.

On reflection, the name should have aroused suspicion. *Prism Me a Lie Tell Me a Truth: Tehelka as Metaphor* sounds long-winded, pretentious and difficult to understand. The book is very similar. Madhu sent me a copy with eleven chapters flagged for attention. She said they were the best. What they contain is reams of unedited interviews which meander unstructuredly, often losing sight of purpose and frequently dissolving into pointless chatter in disconcerting slang. The detail is overwhelming but it doesn't lead anywhere or, if it does, I got lost.

Often the 'voice' of the author is absent but when you can detect it, it appears to snigger or pontificate. Madhu seems to fancy herself as a psychoanalyst but I doubt if her efforts will win accolades. Even when there is the odd ray of sunshine, finding it is damnably difficult.

Chapter 19, on the hounding of Shankar Sharma and Devina Mehra, is a perfect example. It's eye-opening yet it also illustrates Madhu at her best and worst – exhaustive research but a confusingly detailed account. Instead of wanting to read on you're tempted not to continue. Confronted with the howling cries of your weary mind and tired hands, it requires dogged persistence not to give up. By the way, this is a heavyweight book but purely in terms of its bulk!

My efforts unearthed the following nugget. In a long excerpt from an Arun Jaitley interview, unhelpfully printed without paragraphs, I discovered that Tehelka had testimony exonerating George Fernandes but did not reveal it. Whether that's tantamount to hiding is for you to judge but this is what Jaitley says: 'In the absence of any evidence against George and the tape containing a statement that George is a very honest man, editing that out was an act of dishonesty.'

On page 353 Madhu offers a comment. Read carefully and ask if she's fair or mealy-mouthed? Does she accept George Fernandes was innocent and wrongly targeted and, therefore, unjustly treated or does she, instead, seek to excuse Tehelka and gloss over the case against them?

'The slanted editing in removing all reference to George Fernandes's honesty did no service to Tehelka's credibility. In my assessment, poor journalistic judgement, rather than any dark political conspiracy. A common habit amongst us journalists: often the angle of the story becomes so powerful, it subconsciously turns into a motive.'

When I ribbed Madhu about this 'conclusion' she sent an SMS asking me to see pages 483–484. If she had not, I would have skipped them altogether.

And what did I discover?

'Tehelka cut out an encounter' with an honest bureaucrat. A certain Mr Doodani not only refused a bribe but got extremely angry. Again, Tehelka hid this. They behaved as if it hadn't happened. And Madhu's conclusion: 'Journalists habitually fall in love with the angle of the story on which they are focusing and any point raised that moves it away from that angle, is dropped … it made their report appear biased.'

Reflect on the word 'appear'. Does it suggest balance and careful consideration or an attempt to blur criticism and paper-over Tehelka's faults?

Madhu's publisher, Pramod Kapoor, tells me her original manuscript was three times longer. Roli Books reduced 1800 pages to 587. I began by apologizing to Madhu; perhaps I should end by thanking Pramod?

11 February 2009

I Wish I Had Said No

As a rule I never interview good friends. It's a sure-fire way of getting your emotional loyalties and professional ethics entangled. Friends don't want to be asked awkward questions yet if you knowingly desist you aren't doing your job. Either way you're a loser.

But what do you do when someone asks to be interviewed? Is he accepting the risk or is he oblivious of it? That's what happened when Shyam Bhatia's publisher rang to suggest I talk to him about his political biography of Benazir Bhutto, *Goodbye, Shahzadi*.

I've known Shyam for forty-odd years. Although he's considerably older, as journalists our careers kept track of each other long after school and college associations had ended. Amanda, his wife, was my first dental hygienist. The drive to their wedding was the first long journey in our new BMW.

The problem began when I read *Goodbye, Shahzadi*. Though described as a political biography, it contains unsubstantiated personal details that are, at best, rumour and gossip but, at worst, deliberate sensationalism. I feel they're untrue. More importantly, they don't belong in a 'political' biography.

At the core is an account of an alleged interview Shyam had with Benazir in 2003, where she reportedly spoke of an incident ten years earlier when she was prime minister. Shyam claims she described how she acted as a two-way courier facilitating a clandestine and illegal nuclear exchange between Pakistan and North Korea. Whilst on a visit to Pyongyang, she carried in her overcoat pockets CDs containing the secret of how to assemble a nuclear bomb. On the return she brought back the dis-assembled parts of a Nodong missile.

The problem is Shyam has no proof of this. He insists she made him switch-off his tape recorder and promise never to reveal the story during her lifetime. This is, therefore, a case of Shyam's word against those who choose to question it. And given that he's alleging Benazir was involved in nuclear smuggling you can be sure her husband, party and supporters will.

This 'story' – and I use the word advisedly – is both the high point and the weakness of Shyam's book. So, if he wanted to be interviewed, this is what I had to concentrate on. And if the interview was to be done professionally it also had to be done rigorously. Thus professionalism and friendship were destined to clash.

Aware Shyam is a friend, I began delicately. How would he respond if Asif Zardari called for proof? I'm not sure if he evaded or didn't hear. At any rate Shyam did not really answer. So I tried again. You're accusing Benazir of nuclear smuggling, I pointed out. In today's world that's a heinous crime. This time he was quick to respond. In Pakistan, Shyam suggested, she would be considered a heroine. Perhaps, I shot back, but why would she reveal such details to you? You're an Indian, a journalist and not a close friend.

I saw Shyam's lower lip quiver. It was a fair question but, in the circumstances, also a low blow. He could not have anticipated it. At once, I regretted my attack.

Both of us knew there couldn't be a convincing reply. The question was designed to ensure that. After all, why do people make the most unbelievable confessions to the most unlikely confidantes? They probably don't know themselves. But in an interview 'don't know' is an incriminating answer.

Shyam took it like a man. I felt like a heel. Afterwards he was full of thanks and praise. I might have scored but I could barely speak. Although my skepticism has been echoed by the PPP in Islamabad and, even, L.K. Advani, who launched Shyam's book in Delhi, I can't get over the nagging feeling that I've set in motion a line of attack that's snowballed into a problem for a friend. I might have done my job but I've also let Shyam down.

The sensible thing would have been to refuse to interview him. I wish I had. Shyam, I suspect, regrets asking me. I guess we'll both be wiser next time. Meanwhile, I hope we can remain friends.

13 June 2008

It's Time to Say Sorry

Are we responsible for the distrust, even the alienation, Kashmiris feel when they consider their sixty-year association with India? Have we betrayed promises, mistreated our fellow citizens, trampled on their rights and brutally shattered their dreams? Did our behaviour make the insurgency 'inevitable'?

It may seem odd to ask these questions when Srinagar is enjoying its best summer since 1989 but, I would argue, this is one reason why they need to be asked all the more forcefully. Just because the situation seems more normal doesn't mean the underlying grievances have disappeared. And if we don't look for honest answers we could slide back towards the precipice.

In a book called *My Kashmir*, recently published in America, Wajahat Habibullah suggests the answer is yes. And Wajahat should know. A Kashmir-cadre IAS officer, he served twice as divisional commissioner, Kashmir. Since 1970, when he started his career as a subdivisional magistrate in Sopore, he's witnessed how Kashmiris were treated by both the state and central governments.

'The first in a series of blunders,' Wajahat writes, was the dismissal of Sheikh Abdullah's government and his subsequent arrest in 1953. The Sheikh was not just a hero to his people, he was also the main force behind the accession. He symbolized Kashmiri hopes as well as the link with India. Even half a century later, long after the Sheikh's days of glory, Wajahat says, 'Kashmiris look upon his arrest as the first of many betrayals.'

However, it's the eyewitness evidence that Wajahat presents

that is the truly compelling part of his answer. During his first assignment Wajahat discovered that, unlike the rest of India, in Kashmir 'the only active law was the Defence of India Rules, which allowed the police to keep their reasons for arrest and detention secret'. Though designed to tackle national security in wartime, in Kashmir these were used to enforce routine law and order. 'Small wonder,' he concludes, 'that a feeling of subjection had begun to permeate people's minds.'

Whilst elsewhere in India elections provided a safety valve to ventilate anger, in Kashmir they became a means of denying freedom and subjecting the people to unrepresentative rule. Wajahat recounts the four steps by which elections were undermined. First, 'reject the nomination of the opposition'. Second, impersonation during the voting 'with the pliable presiding officer turning a blind eye to fake identification'. Third, 'the ballot boxes could be stuffed with ballots'. And, fourth, 'the winning and losing numbers were simply changed to favour the "preferred" candidate'.

Two developments in the 1980s, Wajahat suggests, made the insurgency inevitable. The first was the midnight dismissal of the Farooq Abdullah government in 1984. At the heart of the problem was the clash between Farooq and Indira Gandhi. 'She considered (him) a whippersnapper who owed her his position.' He sought to assert his independence, hosting opposition conclaves in Srinagar. Wajahat concludes: 'The questionable manner of the Farooq government's ouster confirmed Kashmiri suspicions that New Delhi would only allow supplicants to rule the state.'

The other was the election of 1987, rigged by the National Conference and Congress. Wajahat confirms that the voting in Amira Kadal was blatantly manipulated to ensure Yousuf Shah's defeat, whilst his polling agents 'were imprisoned without bail for months under the state's draconian Public Safety Act'. Today, Yousuf Shah is better known as Syed Salahuddin, the head of the

Hizbul Mujahideen and the chief of the United Jehadi Council. Refusal to let the opposition win 'drove a disaffected public into rebellion … convinced that freedom … was inaccessible'.

Twenty-one years later, can harmony be restored? Wajahat suggests the happy summer of 2008 could be illusory: 'It is doubtful whether harmony can ever be fully restored.' But if we want to try – and we must – Wajahat offers a small slender line of hope: 'It had been clear to me from early on that resolution in Kashmir could come only with the restoration of Kashmiris' dignity'.

With elections just three months away, isn't it time to start? If the answer is yes, I suggest we begin with an apology. We owe them one.

17 June 2008

FF 8282 and I

I wish I had got to know him better. It's not that I never had the opportunity, only that I threw it away. At the time I considered myself above such mundane temptation. I was obstinate, if not downright stupid. Today I know myself better and would readily concede that such men are fun to know. They add colour to one's life, if not value.

So last week when I was sent his prison diary I read it at once and at one go. It's not a great book but then it wasn't intended to be. It is, however, very readable – in fact, I found it unputdownable – although it's not profound and is hardly revealing.

Jeffrey Archer – assuming you accept every word he writes and don't question the image he creates of himself – emerges as a man of incredible discipline, with an eye for astonishing detail, although almost no passion or emotion whatsoever. Written under his prison number, FF 8282, the book is clinical in its precision and matter of fact in its descriptions. But its details do not reveal anything of the author's thoughts. There is no suggestion of remorse. In fact Archer's belief that he was convicted on the basis of a mis-trial is the only mention of his court case. And what it feels like locked up in jail is never discussed. That, however, you can work out for yourself.

The book brought back memories of the opportunities I had foolishly squandered. He could have been the only convict I knew. Now I can hardly claim anything as intimate as that. Still, we did meet and he did once invite me to his home.

It was on a bright spring day in the mid-1980s that we met over lunch. I was invited by Bruce Anderson (now political editor of the *Spectator*) to The Beefsteak, a small innocuous-looking luncheon club just off Leicester Square. All you get to eat is steak and all the diners sit around a large oak table. Bruce was on my right. Initially the place on the other side was empty. But halfway through a gentleman pulled the chair back and, asking if he could, occupied the place.

I didn't recognize him. I was preoccupied listening to Bruce, who was quarrelling with someone across the table. In fact, it was only when he asked for the salt that I realized he was there. Even then our little encounter might have ended inconsequentially had Bruce not guessed that I had failed to recognize the gentleman.

'You know Jeffrey, don't you?' he asked as he reached across to shake Archer's hand.

'Jeffrey?' I replied, failing to take the hint. I smiled to disguise my ignorance.

Archer laughed. It wasn't often that he went unrecognized. It was even more rare for this to happen at the hands of a journalist. At the time he wasn't just a bestselling author but also deputy chairman of the Conservative Party. And the Tories were in power.

'Well, surely you've read his books?' Bruce said, seeking to alleviate my embarrassment by deflecting the subject.

I hadn't, although by then I had guessed the man was Jeffrey Archer. But try hard as I did to think of the names of his books I couldn't.

'My wife is a great fan of yours,' I blurted out. It was the truth but it didn't help.

'Which one is her favourite?'

He was only being polite. Perhaps Archer had decided I wasn't worth serious conversation but, once again, I didn't have an answer.

Fortunately Bruce found the whole thing hilarious. 'That must have been a blow to Jeffrey's ego,' he chortled as we walked across Westminster Bridge on our way back to work. Once again I smiled silently. I still couldn't think of anything to say.

I would have forgotten about this meeting except one day, eight months later, Bruce walked up holding out an invitation.

'What's that?' I asked.

'You'll never believe it,' he replied. 'Jeffrey has invited you to his Christmas party.'

'Jeffrey who?'

'Don't start that again!' he replied. I tore open the envelope to discover it was from Archer.

I wish I had gone. Archer has a flat on The Embankment with a stunning view of London. His Christmas party is famous for the Sheperd's Pie and Krug Champagne he serves. It's also a glorious opportunity to meet the Tory establishment. But being a Sunday I was loathe to get up early. So I stayed at home.

Archer never invited me again. Since then I've read several of his books and were I to find him on the same table I would recognize him at once. But, unlike his characters, fate doesn't give the rest of us a second chance.

25 November 2002

What the Story of Delhi Means to Me

For years I've wanted to know the story of Delhi but haven't really bothered to find out. When you live amidst history you begin to take it for granted. Worse, I am guilty of comparing Delhi to Canberra, Ottawa or Washington, as if that were pertinent. No doubt every time I have done so I have known I was wrong but that did not deter me. In my ignorance I thought I was making a valuable point. Until, of course, the one occasion when I got badly caught out.

'Tell me about Delhi,' said the pretty young lady sitting beside me on the Air India flight from London. It was sometime in the late 1980s and I was coming home on holiday. She was very attractive and I was hoping to strike up a conversation. 'I believe it's an ancient city with a terrific history.'

'It is, it is,' I replied enthusiastically but not knowing any of it I could hardly continue. So I tried to deflect the subject. 'It's also a lot like Canberra, Ottawa and Washington.'

'Oh God, surely not,' she said, sounding crestfallen.

'Oh yes,' I insisted but having said so I wasn't sure what else to say.

'Well, I hope you are wrong.'

There the conversation ended. For the rest of the eight-hour flight all my other opening gambits met with a polite rebuff. My lack of knowledge of Delhi had put a firm stop to my efforts to ingratiate myself.

Last week I discovered just how horribly wrong I was. Pavan

Varma has written *The Millennium Book on New* Delhi and last Sunday he sent me a copy. At first glance it looks like a sumptuous coffee table adornment – not that I have anything against them – but as I sat flicking through its pages, admiring the photographs whilst dipping into the articles, I discovered that the book contains one of the most readable histories of Delhi. I now know how the city got its name, the story behind its origins, how many 'cities' the metropolis comprises and a lot else besides. I owe it all to Khushwant Singh. For he has written the article on which my eyes first fell and I have read it – no, devoured it – with gratitude and glee.

So permit me to show off.

The origin of Delhi lies in myth, which is so much nicer than boring fact. Once when the Ganges was in spate – today it's too polluted to make that effort – the river threw up the Shastras. (Incidentally, the phrase 'threw up' is Khushwant's although I doubt if he meant it as a pun!) The site is marked by a temple which came to be called Nigambodh. Yes, the very ghat where you and I will perhaps one day be despatched, hopefully heavenwards. 'This,' adds Khushwant, 'was a good enough reason for our ancestors to choose Delhi as the abode of God. Thus arose the first city of Delhi, Indraprastha, the abode of Indra, lord of the firmament.' Today the Purana Quila stands supposedly at the same spot.

Indraprastha was followed by several successor cities before we came to our beloved New Delhi. The number is uncertain: some say seven, claiming New Delhi as the eighth, whilst others say fifteen. In Khushwant's essay I counted fourteen. They are Indraprastha, Yoginikpura, Lal Kot, Siri, Kilokheri, Chiragh, Jahanpanah, Tughlaqabad, Firuzabad, Qila Feroze Shah, Mubarakabad, Din Panah, Shahjahanabad and, of course, New Delhi. But which was the fifteenth? Irritatingly I still don't know.

However the bit I like best is Khushwant's account of how Delhi acquired its 'odd-sounding name… pronounced by the literati as

Dehlee and by the hoi-polloi as Dillee.' There are several versions. It could be a derivative of the Persian word Dehleez, meaning threshold, because the city was the gateway to the Gangetic plains. Another version is that it flows from the word Daidalas, the name given to the city by the Alexandrian geographer, Ptolemy. However Ferishta, the sixteenth-century Persian historian, claims the name is traceable to a certain Rajan Dhilu who once ruled over the city. Whilst some scholars connect the name to the famous iron pillar close to the Qutub Minar. I am not sure if I fully understand this connection. As Khushwant writes, 'The pillar was designed as the standard of Lord Vishnu and was meant to be implanted deep into the hood of the cobra which bears the earth on its head.' It was said that anyone who tampered with it would be cursed. A foolish Tomar Rajput king, who wanted proof that the pillar was in fact embedded in the serpent's head, had it dug up. When it was, the base was found to be covered with blood. The Tomar king lost his throne and his dynasty died with him. It's a wonderful story but, for the life of me, I cannot fathom the connection with Delhi. Is it to suggest that Delhi is a city of blood? Sadly, at times it has been.

Perhaps one day Khushwant will explain things – and also give me the missing fifteenth name – but even if he chooses to leave me less than fully knowledgeable, the next time I sit beside a pretty face on Air India I shall have fewer problems keeping the conversation going. Wish me luck!

5 February 2001

To Think I Refused Him a Job

I suppose you could say he was clean-looking but that would be an inadequate description. When he first walked into my office I was also struck by his confidence and his affability. It's not easy to affect such poise when you are presenting yourself for an interview. Yet there wasn't a trace of nerves or diffidence in his bearing.

It was the early 1990s but I am not sure of the exact year. I think he had just finished university or maybe he had just returned from one of those television courses in America. Shobhana Bhartia, who at the time was my boss, had asked me to meet him. His father, who I have known since I was a child, had also put in a word. My curiosity aroused, I was eager to meet this young man.

'How can I help?' I asked, once the introductions were over. I meant my question to sound reassuring but I don't know if I succeeded.

'I'd like a job, Sir,' came the firm reply. Asking for employment is never easy. Most of the time you want it so badly your own emotions or tension botch the attempt. But the young man in front of me was in full control of himself. He spoke simply, effectively and purposefully. The use of the word 'Sir' – a habit he still has despite the lapse of almost a decade – was a nice touch of conventional formality. It betrayed no deference or false humility.

I wish I had said yes. I could have and all I would have had to do was telephone Shobhana Bhartia to convince her. It wouldn't have been a problem. But at the time we genuinely did not need an extra hand and I lacked the foresight to grab the young talent fate had offered me before others did. Lack of discernment compounded my initial lack of judgement.

Thus it was that Vikram Chandra joined *Newstrack* and embarked on a career as a television journalist. I would like to believe that *Eyewitness* might have propelled him further and faster but, to be brutally honest, it's well nigh impossible to do better than he has done.

But what I did not know then – and would not have believed if I had not found out for myself – is that Vikram is also a great storyteller. This is not a quality intrinsic to television journalism. Most of us hacks who write to footage and other people's sound-bites merely devise linking sentences. Our language may have structure but it has precious little style. We convey meaning but rarely do we evoke sentiment.

Now read the following paragraph describing the play of sunlight on the trees of the Kashmir valley as summer settles over Srinagar. It's from Vikram's novel *The Srinagar Conspiracy*:

> *It was a summer painted by the sun in a hundred shades of gold. The soft light of dawn touched the treetops with a pale yellow gold, each leaf sparkling with its own highlights. In the mid-morning the brassy gold of the mustard fields waved at the farmers who rejoiced at the unexpectedly good harvest. And in the evenings the flaming red and gold of the sunset over the Dal brought lovers and honeymooners out in the shikaras for pleasure rides, and they sat back in their seats, trailing their hands in the water. It was the perfect experience in a perfect land.*

There's a certain magic in that description which goes far beyond the clever use of words or the profound conjunction of thoughts. It's the magic of writing. It's what grips the mind and sharply focuses the eye when you are reading a good book. It's what makes the pages turn faster. It's what keeps you reading late into the night, reluctant to put the book down even though it's past 2 in the morning. And Vikram has it.

I won't lie and claim I read the book at one go. I didn't. It took me several days. But there was a night when I stayed up till three. That was the night I discovered Vikram's facility with the English language. It's present on every page although there are several where it gets buried under the burden of the story it has to tell. At first I did not realize this but once I did I spotted something else as well. Vikram's language – and therefore his style – is most powerful when he is tracing human relationships. The way he writes of his characters, their little gestures, furtive glances or suppressed emotions, invests them with layers of meaning. Then his words tug at your heartstrings and the pages turn faster.

Where the book is less successful is in actually thrilling you. In fact there would be no need to do so but for the claim the publishers make on the back cover where they call it a thriller. Like Frederick Forsythe's *The Day of the Jackal*, Vikram's book is about a denouement that never comes to pass. The thrill lies in the planning and its ultimate avoidance. Forsythe pulled it off because that's all there was to his book. But in Vikram's case, because he has more to offer, he is, paradoxically, less able to narrowly thrill. At least not in the sense of a thriller.

I would suggest that Vikram write another book but this time of the sort he likes to read. I don't know for sure what tomes lie by his bedside but I can safely guess that a man who writes with such power of description could not be satisfied with John Grisham or Tom Clancy. And when he does – I refuse to shelter behind the silly conjunctive if – it will be a great book.

9 October 2000

A Comforting Thought for 2001

Flicking through the pages of a book can bring back long-forgotten memories. It's like opening the door to a locked room and rediscovering its belongings. They may be familiar but they can also feel new. Old memories are not dissimilar.

Last Wednesday, as I turned the pages of the sumptuously produced commemorative volume marking the 75th anniversary of the *Hindustan Times*, the door to the past snapped open. The book is called *History in the Making* and I strongly recommend it. Prem Shankhar Jha's essay on the history of the *HT* is fascinating. I had no idea it would be so rich and absorbing. But it's the pictures that are truly haunting. There are two I'm particularly struck by. The first is of Jinnah in a rickshaw in Simla with a solar topee on his head and a half-finished cigar in his left hand. The men around him are wearing a fez and seem to belong to a different century. The other photograph is of Pothan Joseph's departure from Delhi after resigning the editorship of the paper. The year is 1937 and Joseph is standing on a railway platform surrounded by Sham Lal and E. Narayanan, two of the other greats of this profession. At the time Joseph drew a salary of 500 rupees a month. Narayanan earned just Rs 180.

I suppose it was the salaries that did it. Before I realized what was happening my mind transferred back in time. As I passed into a reverie I saw myself entering the *Hindustan Times* building for the first time. I was twenty-four, back home researching for my D.Phil., and the year was 1979. It was my first association with this paper.

In those days the editor was Hiranmay Karlekar and as I climbed the stairs to his office my heart beat furiously. I had telephoned and asked to meet him. I wanted to write although I wasn't sure what or even in what style. But I had a commission from the *Spectator* in London and I felt I could also get one from an editor in India. I was, I suppose, acquiring brownie points for my CV. I was investing in the possibility of a future career.

'Come in, young man,' Karlekar greeted me from behind his desk. In fact, in 1979 he was a young man himself but as I walked the long distance from his secretary's office to the chairs in front of his desk he seemed intimidating. I'm not sure if he asked me to sit down. At least to begin with I don't think he did.

'Yes,' he boomed after a while.

I wasn't sure how to begin. Why would the *Hindustan Times* be interested in pieces by me? What possible qualities did I possess to recommend myself? Wasn't I simply trying my luck and hoping for the best? In which case, what should I say? To admit to the truth seemed unwise.

So I did what I often do. I spoke. I started, continued, carried on and on, injecting enthusiasm and passion, contrived conviction and youthful zest, whenever I thought each would help, and, of course, I smiled a lot. I tried to be convincing and likeable.

'Hmmm,' he said from behind the enormous desk. At the time I had not seen anything quite as big.

I waited hopefully, expectantly, impatiently.

'Hmmm,' he said again. And for all I know he probably repeated the sound a few more times. Now what sort of answer was that? Was it the start of a positive response, an indication of rejection or was he thinking of something else?

'And do you expect to be paid?'

To be honest I hadn't thought about it. I certainly had not come to offer my *oeuvre* for free but nor had I any expectations of making a fortune. I assumed the discussion, if any, would be about my capacity to write or the paper's desire to publish my efforts but not about the quantum of remuneration.

'Let that not be an obstacle,' I replied trying to minimize the problem by a display of magnanimity. I really wanted to write and if the only way to do so was for free, so be it.

'Sit down, young man,' Karlekar said, smiling for the first time in ten minutes. His eyes also smiled, although at the time I was too nervous to notice. In the weeks that followed, I learnt to judge his moods by those revealing liquid pods.

'Never undersell yourself and never offer to write for free.' He sat back in his chair and looked up at the ceiling. As I would later discover that was another habit.

'If we publish anything you write, we'll pay at the same rate we pay everyone else. Is that okay?'

Of course it was. There was no way I was going to dissent. And so my career in journalism began. Over the next six months – it was a long spell of research and the *Hindustan Times* was an inviting escape from the damp and dark innards of Sapru House library – I wrote frequently. My ramblings – for that is what they were – ranged from domestic controversies to pompous thoughts on Britain, visits to Afghanistan and a juvenile attempt to understand Pakistan.

After a bit Karlekar asked me to write leaders. I was stunned. I'd never done one before and I wasn't confident that my opinions were worthy of such treatment. No doubt I expressed myself freely, even strongly, but to put all that down in a leader and expect people to read it and possibly respect it was different.

I should have demurred but instead I said yes. I've never missed an opportunity and when it is gifted – as this was – I grab it. In time Karlekar offered me the use of one of the assistant editor's cabins located on the paper's prestigious second floor. It was meant as a grace and favour offer but I embraced it totally. I stopped visiting Sapru House altogether and instead would while away the day at the *HT*. It felt great.

Of course, not a word I wrote ever made it to the top of the leader column. Usually mine was the third throwaway piece. But on a few occasions I crept up to second position. On 1 January 1980 – a Sunday, if my memory is correct, and the first after Mrs Gandhi's election victory – I woke to read myself pontificating both from this centre point as well as from the columns of the op-ed page. Nothing has given me a greater sense of achievement. I think that's probably true even today.

Six months later my research ended and I returned to Oxford. I could never have imagined that after a decade – virtually to the day – I would be back at work in the *HT* building, this time a proper employee, with a legitimate office and a secretary all to myself. At the time few people knew of this earlier association.

Today I suspect the number is probably negligible. In fact, until the pictures in the *Hindustan Times* commemorative volume reminded me, it had slipped my mind. But I now realize that I've been writing for this newspaper for twenty years and a little bit more. I feel good about that.

23 December 2000

Secrets from the Past

I had no idea a diary could be so fascinating. To be honest, I've never kept one, I haven't read many and I didn't finish Anne Frank's. But at the moment I'm engrossed in Field Marshal Ayub Khan's. It's a 599-page book sent by his son Gohar. Even though it's published thirty-three years after Ayub's death, I have to admit I'm hooked.

Let's start with the pictures. There are 110 but what stands out in each and every one is how dashing, well-dressed and suave Ayub was. These days few officers are gentlemen or vice-versa but Ayub was definitely both. My favourites are of him shaking hands with Mao, standing in a shark's skin dinner jacket beside Ike, sitting at the Elysee with de Gaulle, striding out with Jackie Kennedy and patting Lyndon Johnson on the cheek. As a general's son I can tell you they don't make them like this any more!

However, it's the political revelations that are spellbinding. Although I'm still skimming through the book I've already come across seven different references to intelligence leaks from India. If they're credible – and why would a man lie to his diary, particularly if what he's confiding is not for immediate publication – India, it would seem, was a leaky sieve.

Read the entry for 1 July 1967: 'We are now in full possession of India's plans of attack against East and West Pakistan.' Or this from 12 April 1968: 'The Director of Military Intelligence came to see me and showed a copy of the latest Indian plan of attack ... (its) well-made and is designed to bring overwhelming force against us

... we shall have a hard task in meeting this challenge.' And then, a few months later, on 16 July: '(General) Akbar showed me a copy of the offensive plan of the 1st India Corps against West Pakistan. It has been marked out in great detail, right down to the battalion, especially the crossings and bridges over the Ravi.'

Even when India discovered that Pakistan had details of its war plans, Ayub's diaries show that Pakistan found this out as well. This is what the field marshal writes on 11 October 1967: 'The Director of Intelligence brought me certain documents indicating that the Indians had become suspicious that we have some inkling of their plan of attack on West Pakistan. They had, therefore, changed their plan, but told their commanders to continue simulating the original plan for the purpose of deception'. It seems our defence ministry and army headquarters were riddled with Pakistani spies!

Two years ago, Ayub's son, Gohar, claimed his father had given him the name of an Indian director of military operations from the 1950s who had sold the country's war plans to the Pakistanis for 20,000 rupees. At the time this was dismissed as a silly, if not pathetic, lie. However, a few journalists like me tried to take Gohar Ayub Khan seriously. We quizzed him about the six officers who had served as DMO in that decade. They were brigadiers Manekshaw, Daulet Singh, R.B. Chopra, K.S. Katoch, D.C. Mishra and Amrik Singh. But Gohar Ayub Khan refused to name the one. If I recall correctly, Pranab Mukherjee, who was then defence minister, dismissed the allegation as laughable. But now I wonder. Does Gohar know something we don't?

Equally absorbing are Ayub's opinions of Zulfiqar Ali Bhutto. He was just twenty-nine when Ayub made him minister of commerce. Bhutto rose to become foreign minister before he was sacked in July 1966. The diaries suggest Ayub was both fascinated and repelled by him.

Ayub says Bhutto was sacked because 'he started drinking

himself into a stupor and led a very loose life'. Calling him 'a clown', Ayub recounts how he discovered after their parting that 'he (Bhutto) had volunteered to spy for the USA'. A few days after Bhutto took over as president of Pakistan, Ayub predicted he would 'come a cropper … in any case the government will be that of the goondas, for the goondas'.

No less fascinating is Ayub's portrait of Yahya Khan. This 'loyal' army chief was plotting to replace the field marshal and succeeded: 'If it was not for his treachery, the agitation (which forced Ayub's resignation) would have been controlled'. There's definitely a lesson here for General Musharaf!

Ayub writes that Yahya indulged in 'big corruption, which was carried on by him through Alvi of the Standard Bank'. Finally, Yahya Khan 'attempted suicide twice but his brother, who lives with him, managed to save him in time'.

Writing a month before the outbreak of civil war in East Pakistan, Ayub says: 'The best solution would be to withdraw the army … and to think about a confederation … we've gone beyond the stage of a federation'. On 16 December, after Niazi agreed to surrender to Jacob, Ayub unemotionally comments: 'The separation of Bengal, though painful, was inevitable and unavoidable … I wish our rulers had the sense to realize this in time and let the Bengalis go in a peaceful manner instead of India bringing this about by a surgical operation'.

I don't know of any Indian politician who has kept as forthright and fulsome a diary. If any had, I wonder what we would have learned?

4 May 2007

History or His Story?

Was Jinnah the cause of partition or did the British think of the idea first? Did the Muslim League push inexorably for partition or did the Congress leave it with no other option? Ultimately, was it individuals who determined the partition of the sub-continent or was it done by the 'Great Game' of politics? These are questions that we in India have hesitated to ask or, when we have, we haven't answered fully or even truthfully. Now, however, they have been posed – and rather forcefully – by a new book that I'm in the middle of reading and find difficult to put down. Yet it's not the questions that are irresistible so much as the answers.

In *The Untold Story of India's Partition*, Narendra Singh Sarila, who was once Lord Mountbatten's ADC, has dug out evidence and stitched together an analysis that provides a very different insight into the developments that led to independence and partition compared to what we have been told. I'm not a historian or, to be honest, even knowledgeable about this period so I cannot provide a definitive opinion. I leave that for others to do. But as a journalist – with a nose for the interesting – I can sniff out a good story. And this is one.

Sarila reveals that the idea of partition owes as much to the British desire for a foothold in the subcontinent to secure their defence and political interests after independence as it does to Jinnah's perception of what suited the Muslim minority or, if you are a cynic, his ambition. He offers a welter of evidence from British documents to substantiate this.

First, Lord Wavell realized that after India's independence 'the breach to be caused in Britain's capacity to defend the Middle East and the Indian Ocean area could be plugged if the Muslim League were to succeed in separating India's strategic northwest from the rest of the country'. Thereafter a succession of military advisers, including General Leslie Hollis and Field Marshal Montgomery, realized the utility of an independent pro-western Pakistan to Britain's defence and political interests. 'From the broad aspect of Commonwealth strategy,' wrote Field Marshal Montgomery, 'it would be a tremendous asset if Pakistan, particularly the northwest, remained within the Commonwealth. The bases, airfields and ports in northwest India would be invaluable to Commonwealth defence.' Certainly, Winston Churchill seemed to agree with this. More surprisingly, Ernest Bevin, foreign secretary in Clement Attlee's Labour government that gave India independence, perhaps concurred as well.

Sarila shows that Jinnah quickly realized the advantage such thinking offered him and fashioned his policies to build on it. He used every opportunity to reassure the British of his loyalty and the supportive pro-western position Pakistan under his leadership would adopt. In fact, Sarila claims that, as far back as 1938, the British position 'was not lost on Jinnah'. As he comments: 'This development marked the beginning of the policy of "mutual support" between Jinnah and the British, which had far-reaching consequences for India.'

It was this burgeoning coalition of interests – not yet, if ever, a full-fledged relationship – which Congress policies, wittingly or unwittingly, further promoted. Sarila argues that by asking its provincial ministries to resign in 1938, the Congress cleared the deck for Jinnah to cosy up to the British, who, in contrast, came to look upon the Congress as if it were a party of deserters. In a sense, this happened again when the Congress spurned the

Cripps offer in 1942. As he puts it: 'If Congress Party leaders had used the Cripps proposal to get into the seats of power in the provinces and the Centre, there was a reasonable chance they could have turned the tables on Churchill,' who was determined to deny India independence. Had that happened, it's arguable that a united India might have succeeded British rule rather than a partitioned subcontinent.

Sarila's book does two things which I find fascinating. First of all, it illuminates certain turning points when, in fact, our history failed to turn. These are therefore moments of 'if only' reflection. They hint at what could have been if a different course had been taken. Secondly, in doing so Sarila sheds a contra-factual light, although, to be honest, it doesn't shine very far or illuminate very much. But it does hint and provocatively so!

This book is compelling reading for interested laymen. But I wonder what informed historians would make of it? Sadly, in India, rarely, if ever, do we get to find out.

27 October 2005

It's Not Easy to Understand Mrs Gandhi

Mrs Gandhi is back in the news. No, not Sonia and certainly not Kasturba but the one we always knew as Mrs Gandhi. The original one and, for me, the only one: Indira Gandhi. Katherine Frank's biography has drawn attention to her alleged love life. To be honest, the book does so only in passing and in the briefest of detail. But for many Indians that will be enough to spark interest and possibly ignite controversy.

I have read the book and at no point was I convinced of the alleged affairs. They may have happened and then again they may not have. I won't say they do not matter nor that the book has no business to discuss them. It's a biography and the loves of your subject are a legitimate part of any biographer's subject matter. It's just that we don't know enough to conclude either way. Nor does Katherine Frank herself. She accepts that what she is purveying is the gossip of the day. It's worth knowing – and I am not so puritan as to be shocked by any of it – but I wonder if in publishing gossip – even if you admit it's no more than that – you don't end up giving it credence and credibility?

It's a dilemma Ms Frank would undoubtedly have faced. Should she have left out the stories and left her book incomplete or included them and run the risk of conferring a plausibility they do not merit?

I don't pretend to know the answer but the question is well worth asking. Yet the sad part is that this biography – a very competent and readable one even if a bit inadequate in its political analysis – will be submerged by the different answers to just this one question. Everything else will be ignored and a lot else about Indira Gandhi will remain forgotten.

So today I want to share my reminiscences of a woman who straddled our lives for the best part of twenty years. I make no special claim to understand her nor have I known her very well. But we did meet and I do have memories. They suggest a woman that is far more colourful and far more interesting than the commonplace image of her or even the many biographical sketches we have been given. I shall draw no conclusions but I think they might be obvious.

❀ ❀ ❀

I think it happened at about 11 a.m. It was a winter morning in January or February. The year was 1976. The Emergency was about six months old. My sisters and I were breakfasting at 1 Safdarjung Road before going with the Gandhis to see a film at Rashtrapati Bhawan. I was particularly excited because the film was one of the sequels to Peter Seller's masterpiece *The Pink Panther*. It was either the 'Return of' or 'Strikes Again'.

We were chatting over toast and coffee. On a cold January morning one can drink cups of the stuff without noticing. Suddenly Indira Gandhi spoke up.

'Hurry up, children,' she said. 'It's already past 11 and the president will arrive at 11.10. We must be there before him.'

But we were far too preoccupied with breakfast to listen. It was a Sunday morning and no one felt the need to hurry. Although none of us said so the thought must have occurred to everyone at the dining table: the president can wait.

Everyone, that is, except Indira Gandhi. A few minutes later, she looked anxiously at the large wristwatch on her hand and this time addressed Sanjay directly.

'Ring Rashtrapati Bhawan and tell them we will be five minutes late,' she said. 'The president must not arrive before us and be kept waiting.' And then turning to the rest of us, she added, 'And now let's go. You can finish your coffee afterwards.'

In a flash we were off. We arrived before Mr Ahmed but even so Mrs Gandhi made a point of apologizing for having kept him waiting. Later I can remember my sister Premila recounting the incident and pointedly adding a moral to the story.

'I must say I found her concern for etiquette very impressive,' Premila declared. 'Here she is the Empress of India and Fakhruddin Ali Ahmed her creation and yet she was determined not to slight him. I wonder how many other dictators would have behaved this way?'

The anecdote is of little consequence except to suggest that Mrs Gandhi was a complex person. On the one hand she cut every corner to declare the Emergency and then used every ruse to legitimize her power and absolve herself of all wrongdoing in the Allahabad High Court judgement, but on the other hand she was deeply conscious of the correctness of her behaviour to a president who was not just her creation but also used by her as a tool. In this complexity lies any understanding of the woman and of the prime minister. So often in our simple judgements we tend to forget this. There was a lot about her politics that was deplorable – and no, that term is not too strong – but there was a lot about her personality and her charm that was admirable and very winning.

Even at her most dragon-like, when grown men would quail at the very mention of her name, she remained petite, fragile and very feminine. It was a strange contrast. Her image was that of a virago. Yet the physical reality was of a gentle, even harmless though cultivated lady with, in later years, a disconcerting twitch in her eyes. She looked anything but a dictator. Not surprisingly, her conversation could often be far removed from the power politics she played so deftly.

I remember a second occasion when she was taking us to a concert and suddenly, before we left, advised everyone to visit the loo.

'There won't be any where we're going,' she added with a smile.

'Oh dear,' said my sister. I think it was Premila again. 'I better dash.'

Afterwards Premila asked her what she, as prime minister, did when she felt the urge.

'It's tricky,' Mrs Gandhi replied, warming to the subject. 'It's so much easier for a man. All they have to do is pop behind a tree. But can you imagine what would happen if I tried that?'

We laughed. The idea seemed preposterous and yet the problem was only too real.

'I have trained myself to drink all the water I need last thing at night. Hopefully that way it's out of the system by the morning.'

She was a very sensitive but also a hugely fun-loving person. If she sensed that her presence was intimidating her children's guests she would quietly get up and ask for her dinner to be served in her bedroom.

'I think I'm the cause of all this unnatural silence,' she once pronounced as she got up and slipped away. Her boiled eggs (for that's what I think she was eating) followed her.

When her father was the prime minister and the family lived in Teen Murti House, she would design treasure hunts for her sons' friend's birthday parties. Small 'teams' would be organized to scour Delhi to collect the 'treasure' in response to clues she had personally devised. I remember two of them. The first was a fish bone from a restaurant called Alps. The second was a policeman's cap. Sanjay's team won because he alone knew how to obtain the latter. He drove home and asked the guard on duty at the gate if he could borrow his.

❁ ❁ ❁

Let me admit my memories of Mrs Gandhi are very different to those that gained currency during the Emergency. Yet at least one of them is from that period. And no doubt there are thousands of others with their own personal but equally contradictory recollections. Each of us who met her has his or her own image and that often differs, sometimes sharply, with the received wisdom. And yet the Emergency, the Punjab crisis, the overthrow of N.T. Rama Rao and Farooq Abdullah and the supersession of judges was all too real. They happened – all that can be disputed is why. So what do we make of Mrs Gandhi? What was she actually like?

Katherine Frank's book has raised these questions. The answers elude us.

10 April 2001

Another Edwina–Nehru Story

Did Edwina Mountbatten and Jawaharlal Nehru have a sexual relationship? I don't know but I would certainly hope so. After all, if they loved each other as much as Edwina's daughter, Pamela, asserts – and she says Edwina left behind suitcases full of letters when she died – then it would be terribly sad if their affection was not consummated but left incomplete. And now, before you spill your breakfast coffee in moral apoplexy, let me add that I'm only echoing what Nehru's sister, Vijayalakshmi Pandit, wrote years and years ago.

The truth is that even when Pamela Hicks claims (in her book *India Remembered*) that the relationship was platonic, she can't be sure. To begin with, would a seventeen-year-old daughter be likely to know? Surely her mother and Nehru, whom she called Mamu, would have gone to enormous lengths to hide it from her? And, in fact, when I pushed the point, doubt did creep into her answers.

'Panditji was a widower,' I said. 'He needed female affection and he must have wanted it. Your mother was alluring and beautiful. They were so close together. It would be natural for the emotional to become sexual.' This was her reply: 'It could be and maybe everybody will think I'm being very naive... but I don't believe it.'

Well, if it really was the case that their affair remained Platonic, Nehru must have felt somewhat cheated. Edwina had had lovers before. Pamela Hicks readily admits as much. Paul Robeson, the black American actor, was rumoured to be one of them. So if

Nehru didn't make it to the list I, for one, would argue that he had grounds for feeling hard done by.

However, my purpose this Sunday morning is not to wallow in speculation. Instead I want to share a true story about Edwina. One that reveals her gentle caring character as much as her influence on Nehru. And, in this instance, thank God for that!

Sometime in 1948, when Lord Mountbatten was governor general and Nehru prime minister, my Mamu, Gautam Sahgal, proposed to Nehru's niece, Nayantara Pandit, and she accepted. Mrs Pandit, who recognized her brother as the head of the household, suggested that his permission was necessary. As my grandfather was unwell it fell on my elder uncle, Narottam, to meet Nehru and seek his blessings for the proposed marriage.

Now, Uncle Gogu, as Narottam is known, was barely twenty-nine years old at the time and a mere deputy commissioner in the ICS. The prospect of asking the prime minister for his niece's hand was daunting. It filled him with understandable trepidation. What if the old boy said no? Would Gautam ever forgive him?

Uncle waited till Nehru visited Simla. An appointment was sought at the Retreat in Mashobra, where Nehru was staying with the Mountbattens. Uncle Gogu, visibly nervous, arrived early. Fortunately it was Edwina who first met him.

'Don't be nervous', she said encouragingly, 'Let's have a cup of coffee together and then I'll take you to see the Big Man.' It didn't take Uncle long to realize Edwina knew everything.

Her obvious warmth settled Uncle's nerves. Later, when she escorted him into the study, where Nehru was sitting, his chin cupped in his hands, staring at the distant mountains, she stayed on to ensure all started well.

'Edwina's presence seemed to soften Nehru,' Uncle recalls. After a while, having put him in the right mood, she quietly slipped out. What followed was a long lecture on socialism. Uncle Gogu listened attentively although he passionately disagreed. Neither then nor now does he accept Nehru's views. His patience, however, was rewarded with Nehru's willing permission for the marriage.

On his way out Uncle Gogu met Edwina again. She was waiting just in case things took an unexpected turn. This time her smile and conspiratorial wink were perfect confirmation that she had persuaded the prime minister of India to give the right answer.

Of course one can't judge an entire relationship by one little incident, but I suspect Edwina Mountbatten was a wonderful influence on Nehru. She soothed his anxieties, softened his irritability and helped him come to sensible, practical decisions.

Pamela Hicks told me how Nehru's love had made her mother a happier person. 'It made my mother, who could be quite difficult at times, as many very extraordinary woman can be... lovely to be with.' I'm confident it was equally true the other way around. Uncle Gogu, I feel sure, would agree.

20 July 2007

Chapter 9

Dropping In

'Mornin Guv.'

Long Live London!

I've just returned from a weekend in London, a city I consider the most civilized in the world. But before you start spluttering into your coffee, consider carefully the adjective I've used. Not the most beautiful, certainly not the cheapest and by no means the most efficient or polite. And yet, despite these minor negatives, without doubt the most civilized.

So what do I mean by civilized and what are the qualities that put London at the top of that list?

Civilized is not just heritage and history, not merely culture, and it's a lot more than manners and behaviour. To be civilized a city has to also be accommodating. London most certainly is. You don't have to be English or even British to belong. You don't have to be Anglo-Saxon or even Caucasian to fit in. You don't have to be Christian to feel at home. London is truly multicultural, multi-ethnic and multi-religious.

Actually, London is a microcosm of the world. Oxford Street is witness to almost every nationality, skin colour, sex and dress-style known to man, woman or transgender. Some may look exotic in Paris, several would be out-of-place in New York and many would jar in Berlin but in London they simply blend together. They belong.

So, now, let's tackle the second question. What is it about London that is a magnet to this multitude? What are its unique qualities that attract across the divide of creed, caste, community and class?

To begin with, London has the best of everything – television, theatre, museums, restaurants, shopping, even newspapers and magazines. And it's within easy access of the most stunning countryside and heritage homes. Samuel Johnson wasn't joking when he said, 'If you're tired of London, you're tired of life.'

The second quality is the English language. Despite their frequently frightful accents, everyone in London speaks English. That's certainly not the case in Paris, Berlin, Tokyo or Milan. Indeed it's not even true of New York or Los Angeles! And the ability to speak and be understood without flapping your hands or pulling your hair is a boon that can only be appreciated when it's denied. Spend a day in Paris and you'll see how exasperating it is not to be able to communicate. What's worse is the locals speak English but won't.

However, it's the third quality that is the most important of all. It's the Britishness of the Londoner – and here I mean the natives – that makes the city truly special.

I'm talking of two characteristics – the British stiff upper-lip and their sense of privacy. No matter what happens, they don't make a fuss. They underplay everything. If you spill red wine over a damask tablecloth, your hostess won't get into a tizzy. If you prang your car into the one in front the guy won't start a fight. If you stumble out of a pub and puke all over the pavement, no one will shout at you. They'll simply step aside and move on.

And Londoners don't care about who you are or what you're doing. You can skateboard down Ken High Street with Mohican hair dyed green and no one will stare at you. Or you can flounce out of a Bentley in a flowing agbada with the biggest turban on your head and the doorman at Harrods will greet you with the same cheery 'Mornin Guv' he uses for everyone else. Indeed, if you're a stunning woman with very little on, London is the last place to attract attention. The less you wear the more they look away. Nothing shocks them.

But they are – and poor Queen Victoria got it horribly wrong – frequently amused. They have the best sense of humour and a great capacity to laugh things off. Their jokes are clever, subtle and frequently self-inflicted. There's nothing they won't laugh at or joke about. The queen is the favourite butt and she wouldn't have it otherwise.

Now, tell me, where else in the world can you find this collection of qualities? And if London is the only answer, isn't it the most civilized city in the world?

20 March 2008

Anyone for a Singapore Sling?

It's a shame one arrives in Singapore feeling sleepy. As a result you don't appreciate the drive into town. Yet it's one of the most strikingly beautiful journeys from airport to city centre that I can recall. The dual carriage way is lined with trees, hedges, tropical plants and a profusion of shrubs. But what's truly amazing is the careful topiary. The trees are only allowed to grow to a certain height and are designed to spread in a particular way. The bushes are cropped and meticulously shaped. And the turf on the verge is perfectly manicured.

In Delhi one would pay a fortune for a private garden that looked similar. Even then it would probably be impossible to achieve. In Singapore the city authorities have done it for everyone to view. The least the airlines can do is change their schedules so you can enjoy some of this.

❋ ❋ ❋

Looks can be deceptive and perhaps this time they are. The downtrend in the information technology industry is worrying Singaporeans though few talk about it.

I'm told that in the last half decade the Island's senior minister, as Lee Kuan Yu is called, pushed Singapore to invest heavily in IT. It was his bid for the twenty-first century. In the '60s and '70s, he made the Island a free trade zone well before his neighbours realized he was stealing a march on them. In the '80s, he made Singapore the Asian financial hub and again took the region by surprise. When in the '90s he plumped for IT, it was seen as another bid to get ahead. Today the question is: now what? There is a question mark over Singapore's future but few have as yet spotted it.

I suspect it will disappear without doing too much damage. But at the moment it adds a little frisson to this otherwise stable and boringly successful society.

❁ ❁ ❁

Actually, Singapore is not boring or, to be more accurate, not as boring as it used to be and certainly not as boring as you may have been informed.

'It's like the inside of an efficient hospital,' I was told when I first visited twelve years ago. 'Clean, clinical, sanitized and sterile.'

Clean it still is and efficient it can't help being. But it's no longer sterile and it's certainly not static.

'You looking for a bit of fun, Sir,' said the taxi driver when I asked to be taken to Orchard Road. My intention was to head for the shops. After all, shopping is a priority in Singapore.

'Yes,' I stammered, although I don't think of shopping as fun. More as an obsession I can't resist even though I love buying things and look forward to doing so when I am back in Delhi, where there is precious little to buy. But I wasn't sure what else to say. I couldn't believe a Singapore taxi driver might have anything else in mind.

'Well,' he continued. 'Where to?'

'Orchard Road,' I repeated. The address is well known for its large and fancy departmental stores.

'Of course, but which end?'

'What do you mean?'

'Put it like this,' he said smiling broadly as he eyed me through his rear-view mirror. 'At one end you spend a lot and get gypped. At the other end you spend almost as much and get unzipped. What's your preference?'

❀ ❀ ❀

I had come as the guest of Jonathan Hallett of Television Asia, the well-known trade magazine that strives to put Asian television on par with its competitors in the west. Jonathan is the moving force behind the Asian Television awards. Having benefited twice from his generosity, it was time to return the favour. This time I was present as a judge.

It was an eye-opening experience in every sense of the term. Like most Indians, I suppose, I am guilty of the presumption that our television is amongst the best in Asia. We're free, outspoken, innovative and very quick to respond. Well, so is everyone else except they also bring another quality into play. Their emotions. Not in the sense of prejudice but in the sense of passion. The result can be riveting.

Alongside other sections I was part of the panel judging the best documentary award. There were two entries that literally took my breath away. The first was from the Philippines on the people's power movement that replaced Estrada with Macapagal-Arroyo earlier this year. The second was from Korea and focussed on the first meeting between divided families after a painful partition of fifty years.

The panel sat in pin-drop silence as both were played. Not a person coughed. No, I don't even think anyone moved or crossed their legs. It was hypnotic.

The first ended amidst spontaneous applause. We felt part of the triumph the documentary sought to portray. The second left everyone in tears. I sobbed uncontrollably. But then I often do. Even Bollywood films leave me crying. This time, however, so was everyone else.

Consequently it became a tough choice to pick the winner. After all, which is the more difficult emotion to evoke: joy as you watch someone else's triumph or pain and sorrow as you identify with their suffering?

Try and answer that question. It's not easy.

* * *

You don't realize how good coffee can taste until someone serves you a decent brew or – and this may sound odd but it's the truth – until you visit Starbucks.

Until two years ago the very name would put me off. I can't say why but it sounded cheap and nasty. I've walked past countless Starbucks shops in London with my nose superciliously in the air. I'd smile when others praised the place as if to suggest I knew better. Yet all along I was wrong and horribly so.

Then, in 1999, I had a Starbucks coffee. It was an ordinary Cafe Mocha but it was mind-blowing. No, that's not an exaggeration because at first sip it blew my prejudices away. I asked for a second cup and only the thought I might seem greedy stopped me asking for a third. But I regretted it.

So last weekend I had plenty of Starbucks, if I can put it like that. Every time my concentration seemed to wander Jonathan would suggest another and I was disinclined to refuse. Ultimately, it was the size of my bladder that stopped me having more. But I'm working on that.

I now hope that one of the rich entrepreneurial barons who occasionally read this column will take a hint and introduce India to Starbucks. They've given us Dominos, McDonalds, Pizza Express and Baskin Robbins. Surely Starbucks has to be next?

24 September 2001

Paradise Regained

I clearly remember my first visit to Sri Lanka. It was the winter of 1986, Jayawardane was in his second term as president and Premadasa was prime minister. The Tamil struggle was in its infancy.

As the incoming plane flew low over the lush fields of Katanayake, glinting in the bright sunshine, I could tell why this island was once called Serendip. From the sky, its beauty is dazzling: acres and acres of brilliant emerald green edged by the deep azure blue of the sea.

The first thing that strikes you is the people. In the 1980s they always seemed to smile. More than that, they laughed easily and, usually, they laughed a lot. Consequently, they were easy to approach, willing to chat and went out of their way to help. Rukman Senanayake, a nephew of the former prime minister, took me to Kandy and Nuwara Eliya, cracking jokes about the Sri Lankan accent all the way.

'Pay close attention to our pronunciation,' he teased. 'We call it the Temple of the Tooth!' He was talking about the famous temple with the Buddha's tooth, except his pronunciation made the word rhyme with foot. It was our first meeting but it felt as if we'd known each other for years.

The next two decades did a lot to wipe the smile off Sri Lankan faces. After successive onslaughts of LTTE terrorism, their jovial innocence evaporated. Instead, a look of tired resignation and a philosophical nodding of the head appeared to take its place.

For me the most telling experience was with a taxi driver in 1997. We were driving to the Hilton, hours after the hotel had been bombed by the LTTE. I was one of a hundred-odd victims. With bandages on my head, hands and shin, I was returning to pick up any bags.

The drive began in companionable silence. Although he couldn't bring himself to speak, the driver kept sucking his cheeks and shaking his head in evident sympathy. But as the devastated hotel came into view his restraint vanished.

'What a terrific hotel this used to be.' He spoke softly, with evident pain. His eyes were wet. 'I remember all the happy people I have brought here. Will they ever come back?'

'Of course they will.' I tried to be reassuring although I was about to leave, lucky to have survived the LTTE. 'The future will be bright.'

'The future?' I've never heard the word spoken with so much disbelief. He said no more yet he had said it all. The silence that followed was pregnant with despair and hopelessness.

Sri Lanka, I suddenly realized, had lost its future. It only seemed to have a past. It had become an island of memories. With each passing year they became both exaggerated and faded. But because that's all that was left they were clung to tenaciously.

I may be exaggerating a little, but that future has returned to the horizon with the defeat of the LTTE. Whilst their struggle for Tamil rights was undoubtedly fair and just, the Tigers had become an insuperable obstacle to the success of their own cause. They may have seen themselves as freedom fighters but millions perceived them as murderers and terrorists. They had transformed into their own enemies.

The challenge now is to win over the hearts and minds of the Tamil people. That sounds like the most trite of cliches but the truth often is. The test is not the political system President Rajapaksa will offer the north – though that's important enough – but the smaller, more important steps he must take to weave the Tamil minority into the mainstream: real representation in the civil and defence services, effective implementation of Tamil as a national language at the level of police stations and small government offices and the eradication of the attitude that Sri Lanka is a Sinhala country.

Perhaps my taxi driver is smiling today. Maybe he can see or, at least, sense a future. But it has still to be realized. Otherwise, like a mirage, it could vanish once again.

29 April 2009

The Story the President Told Me

Occasionally – but only occasionally – I find out things that are almost stranger than fiction. It happened recently in the most unlikely of circumstances from the most incredible of sources. But for all that the story is true or, at least, I have no reason to doubt it. And since I wasn't told to keep my mouth shut – in fact, I half believe my informant would want me to blab – I'll share it with you. So sit tight and read on.

Last weekend in Colombo, as I stood staring at a rather nice oil painting on the garden-facing wall of Chandrika Kumaratunga's office, she came up from behind and whispered, almost conspiratorially, into my ear.

'Do you like it?'

I said I did. It was impossible not to. Nor was I lying.

'Do you want to know the story behind this painting?'

I stared at her perplexed. What on earth could she mean? Presidents hardly ever presage their remarks with such broad hints of an impending scoop. Yet I had the distinct feeling I was about to learn something special. She obviously recognized my gleeful smile as a way of saying yes because without waiting for a verbal reply she started to tell me the story.

'This painting has hung in this house for over 200 years. It's an old Dutch portrait, a scene from south Sri Lanka. That's the temple at Habantota (or, at least, that's what it sounded like to my Punjabi ears).'

'How very beautiful,' I said.

'But that's not the point of my story,' Mrs K said. She sounded a little irritated at my interruption. 'It's been here from the days when this was the governor-general's house and it's stayed here after independence. About ten years ago it went missing and no one knew what happened to it.'

'Oh,' I said, not knowing what else to say. 'So how did it reappear?'

I half thought this was going to be one of those mystery stories. You know the sort I mean – paintings that disappear in the dead of night and reappear on a bright dawn six years later. A sort of act of the occult. I was wrong.

'Well,' the Sri Lankan president continued, 'one day the gentleman who is at present our high commissioner in Delhi was leafing through a Christie's catalogue. At the time he was vice chancellor at the university here in Colombo. He's fond of looking at auction catalogues. But as he flipped through this one he saw a picture of the painting. It was up for sale.'

'You mean you bought it back?'

'Good heavens, certainly not,' said Mrs K. 'Let me finish the story before you jump to your conclusions. Don't treat this like one of your interviews!'

I smiled bashfully and promised to keep my peace.

'Mr Bandaranayake, that's his name, informed me and I alerted our high commission in London. In turn they contacted Christies. And do you know what Christies told them? They said the painting had been brought for sale by a Sri Lankan gentleman. We asked for his name and it turned out to be President Premadasa's son-in-law.'

Premadasa – in case you're not up to speed with Sri Lankan political history – was president of the island from 1988 to 1993 when he was assassinated by the LTTE. He belongs to the opposition United National Party. Mrs K clearly hates him. She even believes he is guilty of ordering her husband's assassination.

'You mean he stole it?' I could hardly bring myself to ask the question. Sons-in-law of presidents don't steal government property from their father-in-law's official residence. I thought that was a golden rule thieves always honour.

'What else?' And when we questioned him he actually had the cheek to claim he'd bought the painting on Portobello Road for 25,000 pounds.

Now, Portobello Road is where you go to buy antique second hand silver. I've bought quite a lot there myself. On Saturdays the pavements are crowded with dealers up from the country for the day. You can pick up a few bargains but I doubt if an old Dutch master would be one of them.

'I can hardly believe it,' I said.

'Well, it's the truth,' said the president of Sri Lanka. 'You see, sometimes we politicians can tell a story that takes the wind out of your journalistic sails!'

17 September 2001

A Farewell to Afghanistan

The Kabul I remember was very different. In fact, Afghanistan itself was another country. Zahir Shah was on the throne, the hippies had yet to discover the place and Chicken Street was only famous for its crude abattoirs. The birds were kept in open street-facing cages. Once a purchase was concluded their necks were wrung in front of you and the blood drained into the open *juis* (gutters) that lined the street. It was heady stuff but quite different to the drug trade that took over in later years.

Kabul was a happy city. Innocent and carefree but also a little deceptive. Behind the huge walls that surrounded each house, ensuring privacy and protection, lived middle classes at ease with western sophistication. Women smoked, painted their nails and dressed in the best of French fashion although they might wear a *burkha* if they ventured outdoors. Men wore suits and kissed the hands of the ladies they met. French was spoken as frequently as English. And it certainly wasn't uncommon to see people drinking.

My father was the Indian ambassador and we lived on the same street as the American embassy. Except at the time it did not exist. Our house faced a vast open expanse of barren land but visible at the far end was the Pakistan ambassador's residence. Alongside was the home of Marshall Shah Wali, the king's uncle. Such geography might seem unlikely today but in the middle '60s it was unremarkable. It also led to close and lasting friendships. General

Yousuf, the Pakistan ambassador, and Daddy were colleagues from the days of the old British Indian army. Not surprisingly, the families became firm friends. Abidah, their younger daughter, taught me tennis. She would wear a white pleated skirt for our lessons and beat me without consideration for my age. I was nine.

My parents got to know the royal family quite well. Abidah and my sisters became better friends with the princes. There were five of them. When, towards the end of our stay, Daddy had a heart attack, he was surprised by how often the younger princes would visit. 'I had no idea they were so fond of me,' he once remarked. My sisters found it difficult to suppress their laughter. Mummy had to bell the cat.

The king also had two daughters. The younger one, Mariam, was a part-time nurse at Kabul Hospital. Fate was to be less kind to her. In keeping with Afghan custom she married her first cousin, only to find that in 1973 her father-in-law would overthrow her father. For the last thirty years she has lived torn between her parents in exile in Rome and her husband in London (after his father, Daud, was himself deposed in 1978). Her life is a sad illustration of the greater tragedy that has befallen her country.

Of course, in 1964 all of this lay in the future. At the time Afghanistan's politics seemed stable, even placid. My world was my school. Known by its acronym AISK, the American School was a microcosm of Kabul's international society. There were Polish, German, Yugoslav, Iraqi, Turkish, French, Italian, Pakistani and even a few Japanese kids but Afghan children dominated. We hankered after peanut butter sandwiches and rich chocolate brownies. We read Superman and Archie comics. We played American football. 'Aw shucks' and 'Gee whizz' were our favourite phrases. My accent drove my mother up the wall. 'No darling,' she would correct me when I got home. 'It's aluminium'. I can still recall her lips mouthing each syllable as she pronounced the word meticulously. But *aloominum* sounded more catchy to my ears and I was determined to be American.

It was a time of innocent pleasures. The Spinzar Hotel, run by an elderly Swiss couple, was famed for its patisserie. The éclairs were everyone's favourite. However, the younger set preferred the Khyber Restaurant at Pashtoonistan Square. It was large, self-service and cafeteria style but it was the happening place in town. Lemon meringue pie and baclava were the most popular choice. It never occurred to us that they symbolized two aspects of Afghanistan's life that would soon be crushed.

On summer weekends we would head for Kargah, a deep-water ice-blue lake a half-hour drive from Kabul. Here there was always laughter and music. Carefree bathers would lounge in their swimsuits. Bikinis were the rage, suntanning was *de rigueur*. Only the enthusiastic would actually swim.

The nearby hill resort of Paghman was the rival attraction. Rich Afghans maintained holiday villas on its fruit tree lined slopes. On Friday evenings, as the weekly holiday came to a close, sipping green tea whilst a cool mountain breeze blew past was a popular pastime. Nothing much happened nor was it expected to. The pace of life was restful and easy, uneventful but full of fun.

Not all of Afghanistan was equally developed. When we visited Bamiyan the hotel was a poorly converted former stable. For heating we were given the braziers on which the kebabs had been cooked for dinner. My mother's request for a hot water bottle confounded the staff. After much explanation they gave her an old whisky bottle filled with scalding water. But the Buddhas were a joy to behold. As the morning mist lifted after breakfast you could see them standing like strong silent sentinels. To a nine-year-old they appeared incredibly big.

I remember our holiday in Kunduz and Mazar-i-Sharif. The high point of the journey was the Russian-built Salang pass. It cut through the Hindu Kush mountains and what emerged on the other side was a different world. Here the water was so cold you could chill your beer in minutes in the cascading mountain streams. When we set off from Kunduz for Mazar the road soon petered out into dry deciduous savannah. We drove for hours across this landscape with nothing but telegraph poles to guide us. It was jeep country but Daddy's ambassadorial Cadillac covered it uncomplainingly.

I wasn't impressed by Ghazni, Kandahar or Herat. No doubt they are old cities, rich with heritage and culture, but they are also hot, dusty, fly-ridden places and the air smells of sweat. It's fitting that the Taliban should have made Kandahar their spiritual capital.

Looking back on my memories one strange fact stands out. I can't recall being scared in Afghanistan. This emotion, so common in childhood, is strangely missing. I was often scolded, and even occasionally slapped. Consequently, I can remember times of anger, pain, remorse, tears and a lot of sulking. But I don't recall fear. I can't explain its absence. It's simply a fact.

If at all there was fear in our lives it came from the constant anticipation of earthquakes. Kabul, a valley surrounded by the Hindu Kush range, is prone to them. Everyone seemed to have his or her favourite earthquake story and none of us tired of hearing it. But in the '60s, at least, earthquakes only frightened us. They caused little damage.

When I returned to Kabul as an adult in the 1980s, just after the Soviet invasion and thereafter repeatedly till the Taliban took over, I found that this fear had been forgotten. A more genuine one had taken its place. The constant rumble of guns. Now people were truly scared.

I don't know when the Afghanistan I have described passed into history. Perhaps in '73 when Zahir Shah was deposed or in '78 when Daud, his brother-in-law, was removed? But there were remnants that lingered on through the communist presidencies of Tarakki, Amin and Karmal. Even Najibullah's Kabul retained recognizable echoes of the past. Maybe it was with the mujahideen that it finally ended?

After the Taliban, of course, only memories survive.

1 October 2001

Bombay vs. Mumbai

I clearly remember my excitement as I stepped off the plane. It was my first visit to Bombay, as the city was then called. I was sixteen and thought of it as India's most cosmopolitan and glamorous. The trip was a present from Daddy after finishing my Senior Cambridge exams. It was also the first holiday on my own. Consequently I felt grown-up and liberated.

'*Kidder jaane ka*?' The taxi-driver's Hindi sounded defiant but also inviting. It suggested an adventure. No one spoke like that in Delhi. There, conversations were more formal, the grammar more old-fashioned. 'Peddar Road', I replied, and settled in to enjoy the ride.

As we drove to Malabar Hill I tried to imagine what Flora Fountain, Cuffe Parade, Kemp's Corner and Napean Sea Road would be like. These were names I had long wondered about. They had come to captivate me. Each seemed rich with the promise of money and chic, modernity and difference. Collectively they were a world away from Hauz Khas, Karol Bagh and Dhaula Kuan. For me, Bombay was another country.

I first noticed little things. In Bombay men wore shorts and women were often in skirts. The taxis were Fiat 1100s whilst the buses were clean, safe and on time. People waited in queues and minded their own business. And no matter where you ate – Bombellis, a bhelpuri stall or the Zodiac Grill – it was a thrilling experience.

But after a while I became aware of the city's atmosphere. You could literally feel it and it was compelling. Bombay was youthful, fun, busy. Everyone seemed to be dashing around. And, of course, Bombay kept awake at night. You could buy kebabs at Haji Ali well after midnight or sip coffee at the Shamiana even as the garbage collectors swept the city. In fact, you could have been forgiven if you thought Nancy Sinatra's hit '*The city never sleeps at night*' was written with Bombay in mind!

That first visit lasted a week but there weren't enough hours in any one day for all the things I wanted to do. Everything was different, special, exciting or simply fun. Compared to Delhi, the cinema halls were bigger and brighter, the ice-cream colder and fresher, the colleges more exciting and youthful, indeed even the clubs seemed less staid. And where in the capital could a teenager drink chilled beer as the traffic honked by?

Alas, I fear the Bombay that won my heart has disappeared, possibly forever. I won't claim Delhi is better but the city that was a magnet, that attracted teenagers like iron-fillings, has ceased to be. Or else how do you explain the attacks on Biharis for being outsiders, on the Bachchans for speaking Hindi and on shopkeepers for not putting up Marathi signboards? In fact, it seems the very identity of the city has fractured. Today its residents have become Maharashtrians, Gujaratis, Goans, Punjabis or UPites. No longer are they Bombayites or even Mumbaikars. Bombay has become its many different parts. It's shrunk. It's diminished.

I may be wrong but I'd say this process started when they forced a new name on the city. In 1995 Bombay became Mumbai but, sadly, with the name a lot more seems to have changed. Bombay was India's most avant-garde city. It's where Indians flocked to realize their dreams. They said the sky was the limit. Mumbai is simply the capital of Maharashtra. The largest city in India's richest state but limited by its regional identity. It's insular and parochial.

However, this is not a requiem for Bombay. It is, instead, a plea to reverse history. Perhaps the old name cannot be resurrected –

although in St. Petersburg and Volgograd that is precisely what happened – but can we not recapture and re-activate the lost spirit? Must the best lie buried with the past? Does the future have to be different to be better? Are there not a few old values we should preserve forever? Otherwise memories will be the only thing left.

23 October 2008

Buddhadev's Calcutta Is a Different Place

When I looked out of the window I could tell it was raining. Not heavily but a gentle constant drizzle. Enough to turn the tarmac wet and make the runway look unusually black. In contrast, the green fields on either side seemed bright and lush. Despite the grey skies overhead it was a colourful welcome to Calcutta.

I don't think I've ever found the city bathed in brilliant sunshine. Fluffy clouds, cool breezes and the pitter-patter of raindrops beating against the windowpane are my abiding impression of Calcutta. That's why I think of it as a respite from Delhi.

Last week, when I flew in to interview Chief Minister Buddhadev Bhattacharya, it certainly was.

'Taxi, sahib. Taxi.'

The line of touts beside the aged yellow Ambassadors chanted in unison as I stepped out of the airport building. I tried to behave like a knowing local. I ignored them.

'We go where you go,' the man at the front of the line said in pidgin English when he realized my Bengali was non-existent. When that too didn't work he added plaintively 'You no go, we no go.'

I stopped beside a cab that looked like the best in the rank. It was only after I stepped in that I realized I was wrong. It chugged along suspiciously slowly. Every now and then it groaned and threatened to stall. Near Chowringhee, within striking distance of the Grand, it gave up. But just as I decided I would have to walk, the engine started again. So, trailing plumes of thick black exhaust smoke, I drove into the hotel.

'How much,' I asked, anxious to pay and be done with.

'Meter-wise 150, Sir,' the driver said, 'but only 100.'

'Why?' I asked, not believing my ears.

'The pain, Sir,' he replied. 'I make you very pain.'

* * *

Writer's Building is not what you would expect. Admittedly it's large, red, central and it's filled to capacity with people. But its atmosphere is languid, unhurried, even casual. Other than the guards in white lounging outside – who do precious little to stop you – there's nothing to suggest this is the heart of government in West Bengal.

The chief minister's suite of rooms open onto a large corridor. From what I could tell its sole distinguishing feature is a collection of oil portraits of Bengali worthies. I could not identify them so I asked some of those who seemed to be on duty who they might be.

'These are pictures of the good men of the past,' I was informed.

'But who are they?' I asked persistently.

'We don't remember who they are.'

'So they can't be all that good!' I riposted cheekily.

'No, they are very good. But we are very bad.'

'And when will that change?'

'Ah,' the man smiled. 'When the pictures come down.'

* * *

The room chosen for the interview was small. In addition, it was entirely decorated in shades of red. The carpet was dark strawberry, the sofas maroon and even the phones were fire-brigade red. The cumulative effect was claustrophobic.

However, what intrigued me was the accumulation of dust around the air-conditioning vents. These were embedded in the ceiling and when you looked up at them they seemed to be surrounded by layers of black grime. On one of them there were things growing out of the circular openings and hanging downwards. They looked like surrealistic stalactites.

'What's that?' our cameraman enquired.

Nirmal's question was met with silence but that only encouraged him to repeat it. He had no idea it might be embarrassing.

'Fungus,' someone eventually answered matter-of-factly.

'In the chief minister's office?' he asked, unabashed.

'Why not?' said the same voice, somewhat defiantly this time. 'There's no hypocrisy in this regime. If it is dirty outside it's also dirty inside.'

* * *

The chief minister is soft-spoken and gentlemanly. But underneath this easy manner is a sharp intelligence and an uncanny ability to get his way. Within minutes it was clear that he represents the new face of Left Front rule. 'We have to learn from the mistakes of the past,' he told me. 'We have to change or else we'll perish.'

I was amazed by some of the things he spoke about. He's willing to shut down failing public sector companies, he's looking for ways to involve the private sector in areas such as roads, education and housing, he plans to visit Japan to invite Sony, Marubeni and Mitsubishi and he understands that to do so he has to convince them the days of militant trade unionism are over.

He also wants to reverse the earlier Left Front policy on English. 'Children should learn it from Class One,' he told me. 'After all,' he added, 'it's the language of the future.' He carries no trace of ideological dogmatism nor of narrow *bhadralok* Bengali chauvinism.

But will the *apparatchiks* in the party headquarters at Alimuddin Street and the officials at CITU let him do any of this?

The question made Mr Bhattacharya smile but it did not fluster him.

'Initially we may have our differences. There may be debate. But once a decision is taken there is consensus.'

'You mean you will get your way?'

'I mean the right way is agreed upon by all of us.'

Not surprisingly, the slogan he has chosen for his government is 'do it now.' The younger generation of Calcuttans might have a lot of fun with the word 'it' but the message is well understood by the rest.

3 September 2001

Scenes from Srinagar

It is the colours of Srinagar that first strike you. After the drab green of the plains – or dirty brown, if the rains have failed – the autumn splendour of the valley is spectacular. It's like being in the middle of a mellow rainbow.

I don't know which is the best view but there can't be many to beat the gardens of the Grand Palace Hotel. Last week, as I stood in front of its daunting chinars, their leaves rust and golden, looking past the red salvia and yellow dahlias, with the tall auburn poplars in the distance and Dal Lake covered in a thin white mist, I had to blink and rub my eyes before I could believe the beauty I was beholding. Behind me was the deep-green wooded escarpment of the mountains resplendent in its coverage of pine and cedar. Above the sky was crisp blue spangled with the pale-yellow rays of the struggling early morning sun. A Constable landscape could not have been more beautiful.

It was cold and it was windy. But it was the noise of falling leaves, often like a torrent of crackles and crunches, that filled my ears. It's not a sound you are accustomed to hear in Delhi. Our year ends – as perhaps it begins – uneventfully. Up in Srinagar the Gods herald each change of season with a fanfare of colours and onomatopoeia.

❋ ❋ ❋

Unfortunately, the first sight of Srinagar is very different. As you step out of the airport you could be forgiven for thinking you've entered a city under occupation. Tanks and armoured cars (or call them what you will) surround the perimeter. Soldiers, with their guns held threateningly, stare at you. Wild-looking commandoes, with their heads wrapped in long flowing black scarves, strangely resembling human bats, drive menacingly past.

Ashok Upadhyay, my producer, who was visiting the valley for the first time, could only shake his head in silent dismay. Words seemed to escape him. The shock of what he was seeing was impossible to translate into simple language. But twenty-four hours later, when we headed back to the airport on our return journey, he clearly knew what he felt. And he expressed it pithily.

'The Kashmiri people must hate this,' he said softly, staring all the while at the check posts with their evil-looking panels of metal spikes. 'I can't believe there aren't better ways of doing this.'

He's right. No doubt security is important but so too is the message it sends out. Perhaps in some ways that's more important. And one must not forget that although an army needs to be effective it must never appear offensive. In Srinagar, I think, this line of distinction has been breached.

* * *

I'm told Srinagar is almost completely free of crime. And believe me I was stunned to hear this just as you must be right now. Our image of the valley is one of recurring violence, bloodshed, insecurity and danger. Crime therefore, one assumes, is commonplace. Where there's terrorism there must surely be theft, robbery and even rape.

Well, that's simply not so. And none other than the police testify to this amazing fact.

Ashok met an old college chum, Alok Kumar, now posted as the commandant of the Jammu & Kashmir Armed Police. Alok told him there is no need for regular policing in Srinagar. And not just in the capital. Even in the countryside, civil law and order is voluntarily and willingly maintained.

'The Kashmiris are perhaps the most honest people I know,' Alok added. Which, of course, makes the tragedy of their politics and insurgency even more poignant. But how many of us south of the Banihal recognize this?

❀ ❀ ❀

I hope N. Ram takes this as a compliment because that's certainly how it was meant. It may have been delivered with a wink and a smile and the comment certainly had the feel of a carefully constructed witticism but, nonetheless, it was sincere and heartfelt. Often the best jokes carry a large measure of truth.

I was talking to a group of Kashmiris in the coffeeshop of the Grand Palace when the subject turned to Indian newspapers. They devour them for news of the state and then argue and debate over the coverage.

'Which is best?' I asked.

The answer was unanimous. It was also instantaneous. *The Hindu.*

'Why?' I queried. I wasn't doubting their judgement. I only wanted a fuller explanation.

'*The Hindu* is only Hindu in name,' came the answer. 'It actually should be called *The Indian.* It's probably the only truly Indian newspaper we have.'

I'll say Amen to that!

10 November 2003

PART II

Out of the Box

Chapter 10

Political Takes

'Do weak PMs get re-elected?'

Follower or Leader?

Twenty-four hours can change Indian politics. Even as late as Friday night, an assessment of Manmohan Singh's prime ministership felt like an unintended farewell. By Saturday that had changed and this Sunday morning, Singh was poised to start another term as PM. So how will history remember the last five years?

The opinion of journalists, I have to admit, is hardly authoritative or even lasting. Indeed, the judgment of one's contemporaries is often overturned by later generations. But for now it's all we have. So, with a certain measure of hesitation and a loud note of caution, let's venture forth. That Singh was a good man — I use the past tense only to emphasize I'm discussing the five years that are over — is indisputable. Neither L.K. Advani nor Prakash Karat would disagree. Both his charm and his moral integrity were unquestionable.

The paradox is he presided over a cabinet that hardly reflected his virtues. The following were chargesheeted and yet appointed and retained as ministers: Shibu Soren, Lalu Yadav, Taslimuddin, Jaiprakash Yadav, Fatmi. Taslimuddin alone faced nine serious charges. Deve Gowda found him unacceptable. Manmohan Singh chose to live with him. There was even a period when Soren and Yadav were wanted by the police, became absconders but did not resign.

Beyond this, there were swirling rumours about ministers who used office to make personal fortunes. The most mentioned was the DMK contingent. Did Manmohan Singh, as PM, know? Did he investigate and find the allegations false? His silence left one guessing. History is bound to be more outspoken.

As PM, Manmohan Singh gave India four years of unprecedented 9 per cent economic growth. But the policy of liberalization and reform, that won him accolades as finance minister, was only feebly attempted and, once rebuffed by the left, forgotten and ignored. This includes disinvestment, pension and banking reforms, raising insurance caps, easier labour laws and the opening up of retail trade. History may conclude that as PM, Singh identified with a different vision of the economy.

In the last five years, Singh attempted to create a social welfare safety net. The NREGA, the Rs 70,000 crore farm loan waiver, the Rural Health Mission and much of Bharat Nirman falls into this category. Conceptually these measures are difficult to quarrel with. The question was whether in practice they made a difference. Today's results suggest they've brought the Congress unpredicted benefits in UP. If that's borne out the criticism that the money did not reach those it was intended for could be invalidated.

The economist PM was successful with his foreign policy. He took a firm and bold stand over the Indo-US nuclear deal, which won support from journalists and could be remembered as his big achievement. In pushing it through Parliament, he showed decisiveness, courage and a capacity for manipulation. If the first two qualities were contemporaneously admired, history may conclude differently of the third.

Pakistan, however, remained a promise unfulfilled. No doubt events, both in Islamabad and Mumbai, intervened but the question historians will grapple with is, Did Singh forego an opportunity to sort out Kashmir when Musharraf was in the ascendant? Omar Abdullah believes he did.

Finally, there's the question Advani has popularized and which has ruffled Singh's sangfroid: was he the weakest PM India has had? This is difficult not just because it's contentious. It's also less than straightforward and we probably don't know enough.

That he was the first PM who was not the popular choice of his party is true. That he was also the first to accept the pre-eminence of his party president is indisputable. But surely weakness comprises more than this? We need to know how he handled his cabinet, his Left allies and his party president. How often did they force their views on him? Or, to put it simply, did he lead or did he follow?

Do weak PMs get re-elected?

17 May 2009

A Wild Guess?

Perhaps it's the heat or maybe it's excess of politics, but I'm going to make one of those reckless prognostications that make wise men weep and journalists howl with laughter. Worse, I have little more than my gut instinct to back up my prediction. It could seem rational, even logical, possibly analytical but I readily accept it's also questionable, disputable and controversial.

Well, so much for the explanation. Or the apologia! What is it that's prompted this self-effacing preface? Simply this: Priyanka Gandhi will be prime minister of India one day.

But let me quickly add it won't happen immediately and possibly not for several years. And it's what happens in the interregnum that will be critical to her candidature and its success. So now, lured no doubt by my own impetuosity, let me elaborate.

My hunch is we are going to see a messy outcome of the present elections. Whether it's a third or fourth front government, or one that includes or is even led by the Congress or the BJP, it will be weak, short-lived and unable to tackle the economic, political or national security challenges we face.

However, the term *khichdi* falls short of fully describing this experience. *Khichdi* is usually light and easy to digest. This government will prove hard to accept and difficult to swallow. And the pain of endurance will determine the outcome of the next election. That could be as early as 2011.

My guess is that at that point India will vote for a strong alternative led by a personality that has a national appeal and can command attention. And if at that stage the Congress is fronted by Rahul Gandhi and the BJP by Narendra Modi, then the latter fits the bill.

Secondly, the process that brings Modi to power will fracture or shatter the NDA. This means Modi will either have an outright BJP majority or, at most, be dependent on the Shiv Sena and Akali Dal. And I'd say his government will probably serve its full term.

So it's seven years down the road that Priyanka Gandhi will step on to the political stage. It will be the shock of the Modi victory – and, perhaps, revulsion against the man, his policies and their outcome – that will overcome both her philosophical distaste for politics as well as her emotional reluctance to replace her brother.

Convincing Priyanka won't be easy and it won't happen quickly. In fact, she'll have to convince herself – by living through Modi's India, by wrestling with her doubts and inhibitions and by accepting, but perhaps never admitting, that Rahul, the brother she adores, cannot restore Congress fortunes or India's self-image and self-respect. She'll have to convince herself that her party and her country need her.

And now, why do I believe if Priyanka steps into politics she could end up as prime minister? Because she has a magical spark that makes her compelling. It's a combination of charm, charisma, presence, appearance and intelligence. You see it on television, you sense it in her interviews and, if my colleagues are correct, it captivates the audiences she speaks to.

She has one further quality, which is particularly rare. She understands herself and is comfortable with who she is. It's a sort of Buddhist self-awareness and it's reassuring to encounter. It makes you want to believe in her. Yet this is why she will struggle and agonize over becoming a politician but, when she does, this is also why she will rise to the top.

Pause now and ask how many 'ifs' have to be happen for my prophecy to be fulfilled? I'd say three: an unpalatable *khichdi* at this elections, a Modi 'majority' at the next and a widespread acceptance of the Priyanka phenomenon in the interim.

The irony is that it could turn out like the disputed Modi comment of 2002 – Priyanka Gandhi will be the equal and opposite 'reaction' to his own coming to power!

5 May 2009

The Untold Advani Story

Perhaps this is self-indulgence, but I'm going to elaborate on a little footnote in history. Now that L.K. Advani has mentioned it in his memoirs and spoken of it in interviews, I feel I can tell the full story. LKA was not 'the hidden hand' that sabotaged the Agra Summit of 2001. He was its architect. How do I know? I helped set it up although I wasn't 'the intermediary' Advani generously calls me.

The story goes back to 1998. At the time Ashraf Qazi was Pakistan's high commissioner and a close friend. Eager to establish a personal rapport with the NDA government he asked if I would help. George Fernandes was my initial choice and I set up a few meetings, usually over quiet dinners at my home. They worked magnificently. Fernandes and Qazi became friends and learnt to trust each other.

'I'd like to meet Mr Advani,' Ashraf announced one day in early 2000. George Fernandes arranged the meeting and I was asked to drive Ashraf to Advani's Pandara Road residence. It was fixed for 10 p.m. No one else was informed.

Ashraf had no idea how long the meeting would last. 'Don't go far,' he warned. 'I'll ring your mobile as soon as its over.' I sat outside in the car expecting him in half an hour. He stayed ninety minutes.

Over the next year there were perhaps twenty such clandestine meetings. The vast majority were at night. I was the chauffeur and the guards at Pandara Road were only given my name. Soon a routine was established. The two As would disappear into Advani's study. I would sit with Mrs Advani and Pratibha. When their conversation was over they'd join us for a cup of tea.

The only person who stumbled upon this – but I don't think he worked it out – was Sudheendhra Kulkarni. In those days he was Vajpayee's speech writer. His association with Advani was yet to begin. At the very first meeting he walked in, unannounced, to deliver papers but fortunately didn't stay. Two weeks later, when the second meeting was underway and I'd parked under a streetlight in Khan Market, Sudheendhra, emerging from a Chinese restaurant, recognized me.

'I'm a little early to collect a friend who's dining at the Ambassador,' I lied. 'So I thought I'd wait here.' Amazingly, Sudheendhra believed this but thereafter Pratibha insisted I wait with them.

Late in May 2001 India announced it had invited Musharraf. At 6.30 the next morning Advani rang. I was asleep. 'I'm sorry for calling so early but I want you to tell our common friend that he shares the credit for this development. Our meetings were a big help.'

Their last meeting was during the Musharraf visit. It happened after the Rashtrapati Bhawan banquet, close to 11 p.m. Ashraf rapidly changed from his *achkan* into casual clothes so no one would recognize him. Advani still had on the grey trousers of his *bandgala* suit. Agra was the next morning. There was hope in the air.

In the end the summit failed. Ashraf's and Advani's best efforts were in vain but the bond they formed did not snap. There were two further memorable meetings. The day after the attack on Parliament, at the *Pioneer*'s 10th anniversary dinner, Mrs Advani insisted Ashraf meet her husband. He was hesitant to do so. He felt it would be embarrassing. But when he did, Advani grasped his hand and greeted him warmly. 'What an amazing man,' Ashraf said afterwards.

Six months later, after the terrorist attack at Kaluchak, Ashraf was asked to leave. The government gave him a week. On his penultimate evening the Advanis invited him for a personal farewell. It was my last duty as chauffeur.

Neither Ashraf nor Advani were embarrassed by the circumstances. They took it in their stride. Events had worked out very differently to their intentions but they had done their best. When it was time to leave Ashraf started to shake hands.

'*Galle lago*,' Mrs Advani intervened. She ensured the two embraced. Tears welled up in Advani's eyes.

25 March 2008

The Importance of Charm

It was a casual conversation with the prime minister but it made me realize the importance of charm. Whatever else he may be, he's a very charming man. Sadly, that's not a quality I can readily detect in the rest of my countrymen. Most of us mistake it for weakness. Instead we cultivate the gruff exterior.

Mr Vajpayee and I met in the middle of the imposing Ashoka Hall of Rashtrapati Bhawan. I was standing near the entrance chatting with James Lyngdoh and Ajay Vikram Singh. The prime minister entered from the other side and started to slowly walk across. We stood and watched. When he was some twenty feet away I thought I saw him gesturing at me. He used his eyes and his smile to do so. It was a knowing look – in part a conspiratorial nod and wink but also an ah-there-you-are act of detection.

I moved forward. But as soon as I did the PM looked away leaving me feeling very foolish. Had I made a mistake? Perhaps. So I returned to the group I had just left. They smiled generously to put me at my ease.

'*Arre kya hua*?'

It was Mr Vajpayee. He was looking straight at me and smiling. His eyes were twinkling. So this time I scampered across. I felt as if I was behaving like a schoolboy. I wouldn't be surprised if everyone else thought so too.

'*Aap aa rahey the phir ruk gaye. Kya hua*?'

The PM grasped my proffered hand in both of his and held on to it. That's how we stood for the duration of our conversation.

'*Mein sharma gaya.*'

I had spoken before I realized what I was saying. I wanted to withdraw my words but it was too late. Of course, it was the truth but it sounded gauche.

'Aaah,' the PM replied, his eyes growing bigger and brighter. '*To sharmate bhi ho*!'

Honestly, I did not know what to say. The PM realized this and seemed to enjoy my predicament. He waited for me to speak. Meanwhile, his smile got bigger.

'My mother,' I blurted out, 'is a great admirer of yours.'

'*To bete mein kya kammi reh gayi*?'

By now the smile had covered his full face. He knew he was being mischievous but he was enjoying every second of it. For my part I felt more foolish than ever before. Alas that also meant I continued to speak without thinking.

'When Mummy reads something I've written about you she usually calls me a bloody fool.'

I knew at once I was inviting another riposte and the PM was not slow to grasp the bait I offered. This time he laughed as he spoke.

'*Ma galat nahin*!'

I must have blushed deeply because he raised his left hand to my shoulder whilst still holding on to my hand with his right. It was meant to be avuncular and that's certainly how it felt.

'*Mein aapko dekhta rehta hoon.*'

He said no more but I felt his eyes said the rest. He rolled them upwards and shook his head from side to side. I interpreted this as a sign of appreciation. Or was it a gentle dismissal? Either way it was a friendly gesture.

Our little chat couldn't have lasted more than two minutes. Maybe less. But the impression it left behind was indelible. I am and remain a critic of Mr Vajpayee but his charm is irresistible. No one – not even his most ferocious enemies – could deny that.

But why are the rest of us so 'un-charming'? Do we not realize how much difference a little polite flattery, a gentle joke, a pleasant aside can make? Maybe we are not equally witty, and no doubt only a few are blessed with the presence of mind to think of clever things to say, but all it requires to be charming is to be nice and to let it show. Surely, that's not so difficult?

I grant that it's easier to be charming when one is powerful and important. In the rest of us that could be mistaken for grovelling. But then why are those who exercise influence and authority so often awkward and abrupt? Are they rude or indifferent? Or do they simply not know better?

I'm sure each of you has your own answer to this question. But let me leave you with mine. Most of us don't know how to be charming – and very few of us realize what an enormous difference it can make – because few people, if any, have been charming to us. We treat others as we have been treated in turn. That's the real problem.

6 October 2003

Go, Mr Modi, and Go Now

I thought I knew Narendra Modi. Not so long ago I respected him and was grateful for his advice. In 2000, when I was preparing for an interview with the RSS Sarsangchalak, he helped me understand the organization and opened my eyes to its weaknesses. With perfect impartiality he made me aware of the damning mediocrity that has come to characterize its functioning.

'Question Sudarshanji about the RSS's loss of relevance. No longer does it stand for excellence. Today it's mediocre in everything it does.' That's how he started the discussion.

'What do you mean?' I questioned. This was the last thing I expected to hear. After all, Modi is an RSS *pracharak*. I had sought him out as a defender of the Sangh, not as a critic.

'The RSS runs 20,000 schools and fifty papers. But none of these has achieved any measure of national distinction. The RSS is dedicated to social work but Sai Baba, the Radha Soami sect and Panduran Athavale's Swadhya Group have bigger names in this field. The RSS doesn't count.'

I was stunned. Not simply because Mr Modi was being critical. More because he was offering a line of attack that came from within the RSS. This was not the traditional and hackneyed left critique. It was the searing disillusionment of the right. It was new. It was different.

'Ask him about the attendance at RSS *shakhas*,' Modi continued. I could sense his enthusiasm. He was behaving like a journalist.

I liked that. More importantly, I admired his honesty and was grateful for his advice.

'Just look at Kerala. The biggest RSS unit is there but its impact is minimal. Instead, everything the RSS dislikes is thriving. The communists, the church and an economy that is dependent on foreign, not *swadeshi*, funds. That's how irrelevant the RSS has become.'

'Ask Sudarshanji about all of this and you will touch on issues that matter to people like me. It will be a fantastic interview.'

I had intended to follow this advice. But foolishly I started the interview on a more conventional tack. We spoke about the RSS's commitment to a Hindu Rashtra, the Constitution, the BJP's alliances and the Vajpayee government's performance. Then we ran out of time. Mr Modi's questions got squeezed out.

Even though many praised the interview and the press were kind to it I knew it could have been better. It ought to have been different. It might even have been original. Had I found a way of incorporating Mr Modi's questions it would have been.

At the time I thought of Narendra Modi as a man who had the strength to question, the courage to challenge and the objectivity and generosity to share his sentiments across political divides. I can't pretend I knew much more about him. I certainly did not get to know him well. But I felt I did not need to. I liked – in fact, I admired – what I had seen. That was enough.

Sadly it seems I was mistaken. No, that's not quite right. It's not being fully honest. The word 'seems' suggests a doubt or hesitation that is misplaced. The word 'mistaken' feels euphemistic. The truth is I was horribly wrong.

The image of Narendra Modi that emerges from his handling of the communal carnage in Gujarat is completely different. The 'other' Modi is narrow-minded, sectarian, mean-spirited and a prisoner of his limitations.

I can accept that his inexperience, maybe even his foolish personal pride, was the reason why the army was not called out earlier. Perhaps he thought he could handle the situation differently yet still effectively, show toughness but also a measure of understanding. After all, it's not easy to crack down on your own constituents, on those who share your beliefs. Even if tragic, such mistakes are human. They happen often enough.

But when he claims that for every action there will be a reaction, when he attempts to explain the murder of Ehsan Jaffri by alluding to the fact the mob was fired upon and when he finds grounds for paying the victims of Godhara double the amount paid to those who died in Ahmedabad he reveals himself as a moral dwarf. To value a Hindu life more than a Muslim one or talk of mass murder as if it was somehow explicable is not just beyond comprehension – it's hateful.

The man I thought I knew was a leader. He had the spirit and the wisdom to rise above narrow confines, to turn opponents into friends, to win admiration from journalists, to guide and be followed. The man I discovered last week is a mere creature – of prejudice, of petty vengeance, of double standards and forked-tongued utterances.

The first Mr Modi deserved to be chief minister. The second deserves to be sacked.

11 March 2002

Why I Respect Ram

Although I can't be certain I think I first met Ram Jethmalani in 1992. It was the run-up to the presidential elections and he was a candidate. S.D. Sharma and G.G. Swell were the other two. No one took him seriously but then Sharma and Swell were not willing to give interviews. That was Jethmalani's big advantage. He was accessible, likeable and whatever he said made news.

In those days I was executive producer of *Eyewitness*. It was a video magazine although we pretended it was the same as TV. We were better than *Newstrack* but, sadly, not as well known.

I invited Ram to be interviewed and he accepted. It was a wild monsoon morning when he drove into Kamani for the recording. Our set was on the auditorium stage and although we occupied only a small portion of the theatre the ambience lent the event a sense of occasion.

Ram came in a Tata Sierra with a big burly sardar driver for companion. The man's loyalty to Ram was as striking as it was surprising. I had not realized that Ram's defence of Kehar Singh had so deeply affected the Sikh community. I was soon to discover that there was a lot more about Ram I did not know.

'Tell me, Mr Jethmalani,' I began the interview in my best inquisitorial style. 'Why do you think you would make a good president?'

I don't remember his answer at least partly because I wasn't listening. I was preparing myself for the follow-up question. It was supposed to be the coup de grace.

'Why should the country want a bigamist as head of state?'

I was thirty-six and far from being embarrassed by my lack of finesse, I was perversely proud of it. I mistook bluntness for boldness, rudeness for vigour and courage.

I'll never forget his reply. It was unhesitating, honest and brilliantly focussed.

'That's a smart question but not a clever one,' he said. 'It's true I have two wives but both my marriages happened before the Hindu Code Bill was passed.'

'So?' I said, but only because I had to say something. In all honesty I had not thought beyond my question. Smart alecs never do. Ram's quick-witted candour had floored me.

'I treat both my wives better than most men treat their only wife,' Ram added. 'So what's the point you're trying to make?'

I did not know. I had approached the interview as a five-minute interlude of fun. Ram turned out to be one of the most impressive interviewees I had encountered. Instead of showing him up he had knocked the bottom from under my feet.

That first meeting epitomized the best qualities of Ram Jethmalani. No matter what you ask him he's candid and outspoken in reply. Despite their tactlessness – and sometimes their rudeness – Ram seeks out journalists and never runs away from them. And, perhaps most importantly of all, when the situation starts to become uncomfortable Ram is undeterred. He has enough confidence in his self-belief and in his principles (in that order) to carry on. Faced with the good fight Ram is happy to fight on and on. I think it brings out the best in him, even if many disagree.

I have noticed these qualities on numerous occasions. From an interviewer's point of view they make Ram a remarkable, literally an unbeatable, interviewee. But they are also endearing traits. We all warm to men who don't hesitate to accept, acknowledge and even embrace uncomfortable truths.

Ironically, these were also the qualities responsible for Ram's downfall last month. Let me analyse the 'story' as I see it and then you can judge if I am wrong.

Ram believed – no, he was convinced – that Chief Justice Anand's insistence on consultation over the appointment of the new chairman of the Monopolies Commission was an attempt by the judiciary to further encroach upon the territory of the executive. He had not become law minister to simply lie back and permit such trespass. He fought back and valiantly. If you look at the correspondence they exchanged, Ram – in my layman's opinion – won the argument hands down. And he knew it.

The problem was Ram wasn't gracious in victory. He wasn't ungracious either. But his letters to the chief justice made it clear that he was right and the other man wrong. The language may not have been intended to offend – as Ram's critics aver – but it certainly wasn't designed to mollify and soothe. Perhaps understandably the chief justice – or so I'm told – complained to the prime minister and the clock of Ram's dismissal started ticking.

Now throw into this simmering cauldron Ram's outspoken opinions on the new TADA bill, on autonomy for Jammu & Kashmir and, finally, on the unsustainability of the case against Bal Thackeray, and it started to boil over. But that's only because all this happened within three or four weeks of each other. Had fate spread out these events Ram would not have been submerged by them.

I have four personal conclusions to offer. Bad luck as much as bad judgement is to blame for Ram's debacle. His attraction to journalists as much as his blindness to the perils of politics misled him. His belief that the truth will convince his critics betrayed him. And, finally, his refusal to accept that sometimes it's best not to answer – to be silent even if that means you are being evasive – lured him towards waiting traps.

And yet, and yet, and yet ... the if-onlys of politics are the stuff dreams are made of. But then Ram in politics was a dream and it was too good to last. For all his failings – if you want to call them that – we need men like him. Men who have beliefs and convictions, the courage to voice them, the fearlessness to be trapped in pursuit of them, the strength to survive their critics and the good humour to keep smiling all the while.

If only Mr Advani had been able to persuade the prime minister to retain Ram and – if I am going to be completely honest – if only Ram had not been so upset by his dismissal to hit out at others. But then who knows how I would behave if I was sacked from government?

31 July 2000

Amma, Amma

The phone rang the night before I was to leave for Madras. It was from the Tamil Nadu chief minister's office. My heart sank. Normally, such last minute calls are harbingers of bad news.

'Sir,' said a placatory voice, a touch too eager to be the messenger of ill-tidings. 'Madam would like to start tomorrow's interview at 1.30 instead of 2.00.'

It was an unexceptional request. Though I breathed an audible sigh of relief I still asked why.

'It's auspicious, Sir.'

Determined not to let any impediment derail the interview with Jayalalithaa, I readily agreed. Three years earlier, when she first accepted to be interviewed, a Supreme Court judgement unseating her torpedoed my plans. This time, when after much persuading she had said yes again, I was on tenterhooks.

Of all the people I have wanted to interview Jayalalithaa tops the list. She intrigues me. Her convent accent, sang-froid, deliberate manner and glide-like walk are captivating. She's so cultivated, so carefully put-together, she seems unreal.

I was, therefore, both nervous and excited as I entered Fort St. George. The silent army of faceless civil servants, beavering like ants, added to my tension. 'Madam' wasn't present but her presence was everywhere. The atmosphere was heavy with expectation and foreboding.

It was only the freezing cold temperature that prevented those of us waiting from swooning or going into a trance. I've never been in a colder room. My teeth were chattering, or they would have been if I hadn't kept talking. The thermostat was set at eighteen but far exceeded its target.

Alas, the astrological calculations that had determined the interview hour proved false. Perhaps the stars were misinterpreted for their augury went awry. Instead Sod's Law took over. Put simply, that means everything that can go wrong will. And it did.

The trouble began with something as silly as flowers. Jayalalithaa had asked for some on the interview table. So a vast arrangement that stretched from end to end was readied. I balked and refused to allow this huge display to obstruct my view. Instead I placed them on a stool by her side.

What I did not know is that the flowers were not intended for their beauty. Jayalalithaa wanted to hide her notes behind them. In their absence, the papers she carried became visible and, as the interview proceeded, I could see her flicking through them. From time to time she even seemed to look down and read.

I suppose my mistake was to point this out. I don't know why I did it. Other interviewees have consulted papers before, although perhaps not so obviously or frequently. But on this occasion it slipped out of my mouth. Her reaction was instantaneous.

'I'm not reading,' she shot back angrily. 'I am looking at you straight in the eye. I look at everyone straight in the eye.'

Thereafter things only got worse. I questioned Jayalalithaa about Karunanidhi, Sonia Gandhi, her ministers who habitually prostrate before her and press accusations that she is dictatorial yet, in the wake of the May elections, reversed her economic reforms to garner easy popularity. With each change of subject her smile became more forced, her voice more steely and her irritation more obvious. 'I'm sorry I agreed to this interview,' she said and meant it.

But it was when I turned to her belief in astrology and numerology that I sensed I had gone too far. 'Who said that I believe in astrology and numerology?' she retorted, her eyes ablaze. 'You say it. People in the media say it. What is the proof you have of that?'

I realized the interview was going wrong. In fact, disastrously so. In desperation I tried to claw things back. With minutes to go I said: 'You are a very tough person, chief minister.' I meant it as praise but the comment backfired. 'People like you have made me so.'

I felt disheartened. Events have a way of taking over and determining their own outcome. This was happening before my eyes. It was happening to me! Finally, in the last dying seconds, as I thanked her, I stretched out my hand and added, 'Chief Minister, a pleasure talking to you.'

For a moment she stared back implacably. 'I must say it wasn't a pleasure talking to you. Namaste.' She rebuffed my proffered hand, unclipped and banged down her mike and left the room.

'Amma,' I wanted to shout, 'you've misunderstood me.' But it was too late.

28 October 2004

Chapter 11

The Occasional Celebrity

'That look… is, in fact, my memory of Madhuri.'

Keep Kicking, Khushwant – We Like It!

What is it that makes some people special? It could be their looks, intelligence, wit, charm or just their magnetic presence. But in the case of a man I met last week – a man you all know of and no doubt have read repeatedly – it was his endearing, self-deprecatory manner. This man could have boasted, loudly and ceaselessly, for his achievements are huge. He could have assumed airs and pretensions as, no doubt, others often do. He could have been a bore, prattling on about himself and I would have sat still and listened. But, instead, he chose to wear his laurels lightly. He made fun of himself. He laughed and he joked. As a result he impressed me enormously.

'Looking at all you've been: a lawyer, a diplomat, an author, a scholar, an MP, an editor and a gossip columnist,' I began, my eyes twinkling with naughtiness, 'are you a man for all seasons or a jack of all trades?'

'I'm just a dirty old man,' he replied and then Khushwant Singh threw back his head and laughed. 'Or, at least, that's what most people think.'

I had met him briefly once before, five years ago, but I did not know him and I had no idea what to expect. He's nearly eighty-five, he rises before dawn and is asleep by 9 at night. The sign outside his front door reads, 'Please don't ring the bell if you are not expected.' I thought here was a man who erects barriers around himself. Such men either have things to hide or, at least, are difficult to know.

How wrong I was. Just listen to him yourself and see if you disagree.

Speaking of himself Khushwant, without batting an eyelid, told me: 'Somebody said that you've made bullshit into an art form and I thought that was a correct description.'

He said that years ago he had decided 'we are a nation of sanctimonious humbugs' whose practice rarely matches what they preach. It was therefore his ambition to prick the bubble of our inflated conceit:

'Kick them in the arse and they will respect you. I enjoy provoking my countrymen. They are really so smug, so satisfied and not at all curious about anything. I think it's worth provoking them.'

'This riled me very much and I said I'll cock a snook at this. If I drink I'll drink right in the open and stand for drink as my birthright. If I like beautiful women I'll say that they are beautiful on their face or write about them describing them.'

And when, as journalists often do, I asked him how he would meet his maker and what account he would give of himself, Khushwant side-stepped the solemnity of my portentous question with the simplicity and candour of his reply.

'I don't believe in a maker and he won't ask me a thing,' he answered back without a trace of hesitation but a large obvious smile. 'When I die I'll die and that's it. There's no after-life. There's nothing further. Death is a full stop.'

Till then, of course, he intends to go on as he has. So, this Sunday evening, as he raises his customary glass of Scotch, I hope you will join me in saying to him: keep kicking, Khushwant – we like it!

27 September 1999

Dreaming with Kuchipuddi

It's reassuring when people don't change. They may grow up, get fat or become old but when the core of their personality stays the same you still feel you know them. That's how I felt when I met Amitav Ghosh last weekend. Ten years had lapsed since our last contact. In theory, therefore, we were meeting like strangers. But Amitav's unchanged manner immediately rekindled the old relationship. It was as instant as coffee.

'Currybins,' he roared, his face smiling broadly. When it does his eyes disappear behind rising cheekbones. His voice approaches a falsetto.

'Kuchipuddi,' I replied, recalling the name I gave him at school.

We laughed uproariously. Those who witnessed our reunion must have marvelled at two middle-aged white-haired men laughing helplessly for no discernible reason other than they were meeting after a long time.

Instinctively we reverted to nicknames that go back a quarter century. They were last used sitting on the steps of the school pavilion. It was a cold December night, the last before I left Doon. Amitav still had a year to go. This was our farewell. Of course, we insisted, we would keep in touch but perhaps intuitively we knew how unlikely that would be. Time had proved that intuition correct. Yet by using the old sobriquets a bridge had formed across the divide.

Since I last knew him, Amitav has become one of the finest Indian authors in English. The physical change is equally striking. The younger Amitav had a dishevelled Bohemian air. His hair was always undone. Today his white mop contrasts sharply with his deep-brown skin. The effect is at once distinguished and dramatic. It arrests your attention. But he has not lost his habit of looking at you through the sides of his eyes. He does it most often when he's smiling. It gives him a mischievous schoolboy look.

We were meeting for an interview. Amitav was my guest. That meant I had to 'find out' about him, read the cuttings, research, talk to his friends. I was surprised by how little I knew. For instance, I had no idea his had been a quiet, even a lonely, childhood. The garrulous, often loquacious, teenager I remembered seemed anything but solitary.

'I was an avid reader,' he began. 'That's partly to do with my childhood. I grew to distrust the outside world and created my own.'

He was twelve when he read Sholokhov's *Quiet Flows the Don*. It was a gift from an uncle and perhaps his first serious book. Years later he discovered a handful of authors who started similarly. Sholokhov's novel was the link between them. But was it also the secret of their success? I warned Amitav that if he said yes thousands of eager parents might rush to buy copies and their children would not thank him for this infliction. He laughed. 'Serves them right.'

I had read that Amitav wrote his first book, *The Circle of Reason*, in a hot sweaty *barsati* in Defence Colony. Was this the Indian equivalent of an artist's garret in Montmartre?

'Actually it was a servant's quarter!' he laughed. 'Do you know as I was sitting there sweating in the *barsati* I used to think that some day someone is going to ask me that!'

The book is an enchanting journey into the head of its protagonist, a character fondly called Aloo. What I did not know is that the published version is the second draft. The first was discarded.

'It took me a year to write but by the time I read ten pages I knew it was awful,' he revealed. 'I took all the work, all 300 pages, and threw it away!'

He began all over again. Amitav gave himself a year but decided if nothing came of it he would reconsider his dream of becoming a writer.

'So a point of desperation had been reached?'

'I think that kind of desperation, that sense that your life depends on it, either the book will kill you or you'll be able to write a book, that's what puts life into a book.'

Fortunately, the second draft survived. It didn't win instant recognition but secured a firm foothold and he's been climbing ever since. Today he's deservedly successful but the fire and passion have not dimmed. Writing is all he wants to do. Yet he marvels at how far it's taken him.

'I've a sense of wonderment,' he exclaimed. 'To think that my books go out in the world and send back these ripples is for me, in a sense, completely miraculous. I feel amazed by my life. I feel amazed by what happens to me.'

'Do you think it's a dream and you'll wake up to find it's not true?'

'That's the nightmare I often have.'

5 August 2002

A Reverie at a Book-reading

Sometimes when you meet a person you can end up seeing them not as they are but through the prism of memories. In such instances the past overwhelms the present. It's a strange but wonderful experience. Time somersaults backwards, reality converges with history, and myth and legend with truth.

As I watched Vikram Seth read extracts of his new novel I found myself transported thirty-two years back in time. We were both at the Doon School. Vikram was in A-form and in his penultimate year. I was in D-form and it was my second term. We were preparing for the school debating competition. Vikram was the debating captain at Jaipur House. I was the youngest, most inexperienced, member of his team.

'Can't you speak with authority but without shouting?'

Vikram was sitting cross-legged on his chair. He resembled a petite Buddha with sculpted feet and a small round head. His hair kept falling across his forehead. As a result even when he sounded angry he never looked it.

I wasn't sure what he meant. At eleven the difference between authority and a loud voice is not obvious. I cleared my throat, stood up straight and started again.

Vikram closed his eyes. He often does when he is concentrating. But to speak to a man sitting cross-legged on a chair with his eyes shut can be disconcerting. Try hard as I did to control my voice it started to wander.

'You're singing or at least you're sounding very sing-song.'

Vikram's eyes were now open and staring ferociously. 'Remember you won't win any extra points by trying to seduce the judges with your voice. Speak normally, clearly, fluently and you'll carry conviction.'

Neither then nor now do I know what he meant. 'Speak like you normally do' is an injunction that baffles me. If I don't speak like myself, whom do I speak like? Yet when I woke from my reverie it was to find, three decades later, that Vikram was doing exactly that. Of course, he wasn't cross-legged. But the small round head, now slightly balding, was talking clearly, fluently and the audience was transfixed with conviction.

'What an amazing speaker,' whispered Shobha Deepak Singh in my ear. She was sitting beside me on the second row of the Habitat Centre auditorium. Aveek Sircar, Vikram's publisher, was beside her. Earlier, with his help, Shobha had got Vikram to autograph her copy of his book.

'He's just being himself,' Aveek added by way of explanation.

I turned to watch Vikram on the stage but before long my mind started wandering again and I soon found myself tumbling back into the past. This time we were in the Rose Bowl rehearsing for the school's annual play. It was Rattigan's *Winslow Boy.* I was the brutish lawyer. Vikram was directing. The year was 1971. It was his year off between A levels and Oxbridge. It was my last year in school.

Vikram had just explained how he wanted a particular scene done. It was partly description and partly enactment. Despite his lack of height he's a talented actor. Then, with short quick steps and his head inclined downwards, he walked towards the audience stands to sit down and watch. He crossed his legs, cupped his chin in the palm of one hand and rested his elbow on his raised knee. His other hand held on to his foot.

'Right. Let's see how you do it.'

I started. It was the scene where the lawyer cross-examines the young boy. Vikram wanted me to pretend to be angry. Yet the anger also had to sound genuine otherwise the cross-examination would not work. Only after it was over would the truth emerge.

'Not bad. Not bad at all', Vikram pronounced. He was not given to praise easily and I swelled with pride.

Later, rehearsal over, as we walked back, the April night alight with stars but the air hot and heavy, he came back to the subject.

'The funny thing about anger is that it's not the shouting that communicates it. It comes from deeper inside. It's like love and hate. You have to feel it to sense it.' And then after a pause he added, 'I suppose all emotions are the same.'

I returned to the present to find Vikram reading a delicately written extract from his book. Helen is tipsy but excited. Her words are tumbling out. Michael, though detached, is not indifferent. His wit is a foil to her emotion. Their feelings emerge, they grow, they suffuse the context but rarely are they stated.

I have to read this book, I said to myself. I bought it a couple of weeks ago. I like to buy new ones as soon as they are out. It's a sort of one-upmanship I play with myself. But I can be very lazy about reading them. And Salman Rushdie's new novel put me off Indian authors.

A week later I've finished the book but the story, its characters and their world is still with me. Like memories of the Doon School, it will merge into a consciousness that will always be there. Vikram, the stories about him and now his book will fuse into one. I would not want it otherwise.

If you haven't, I recommend you read *An Equal Music*.

3 May 1999

Kapil da Jawab Nahin

I first met Kapil Dev in 1983. It was the morning after the World Cup victory. The shock and the surprise had not yet dissipated. The joy and euphoria were only just setting in. The cricketing world was in a trance. Our winning team was on cloud nine.

'Of course, of course,' he said as I followed him down the hotel corridor. He was surrounded by interview-seeking journalists. I must have been one of fifty. His answer to each of them was equally encouraging and similarly reassuring.

I wasn't convinced he meant yes. Perhaps he was being polite or maybe he was trying to get rid of us. So I started telephoning to reconfirm. I rang the hotel, his room, the lobby, the dining room, his alleged friends. You name the number I must have rung it. Eventually, well past midnight, I got through.

'*Ha, yaar*,' he cheerfully replied. 'It's tomorrow morning at 9 but why don't you let me get some sleep before that!'

Kapil was on time and brought his vice captain, Mohinder Amarnath, as well. They were sleepy, perhaps a little hung-over, but happiness infused the interview. It was the first I handled as an associate producer. It wasn't faultless but it was memorable.

It was this easy helpfulness that struck me about Kapil. Stars can be prima donnas and often reluctant to assist lowly mortals. Not Kapil. This March I encountered the same quality again. We were scheduled to interview Sourav Ganguly. It was the day before the Faridabad one-day game with South Africa. Sourav had agreed, the time had been fixed but he was running late. The clock was ticking and I was beginning to fear the interview might not happen. With stars silly accidents sometimes disrupt the best-laid plans.

'Hi, Karan,' a voice crackled over my mobile phone. '*Mein* Kapil Dev *bol raha hoon.*'

'Oh hi,' I replied, stunned and somewhat speechless. Why was he ringing me?

'*Suno*, Sourav is with me and if you want your interview pick him up from my office in the next ten minutes.'

When I got there a beaming Kapil had Sourav ready, dressed and waiting. The look on my face must have suggested that I was perplexed. How had Kapil swung this? How did he even know about the proposed interview?

'I heard your conversation with Sourav on the mobile, I realized you were panicky and I decided that this was the only way to do it,' he explained. 'Had Sourav returned to the hotel to change you would never have got him.'

So Kapil took him to his office and made him shower, shave and dress there. The interview that followed was a gem but few people outside my circle of colleagues realized that Kapil had pulled it off.

The third example of Kapil's helpfulness was the interview that I hope you saw last week on *Hardtalk India*. When I met him on Thursday the 4th it was to discuss something quite different. The BBC had asked us to do a series of *Face to Face* interviews with great cricketers of today and legends of the past. These were to be personality pieces – soft, gentle, anecdotal. Kapil wasn't very keen. Understandably he had other things on his mind. Yet the idea of an interview to the BBC was one he warmed to.

'*Suno*, *yaar*,' he said, as he poured me a cup of tea. 'Let's do a proper one. You ask what you want and let me answer the way I think I should.'

It took me a few seconds to realize what Kapil was proposing.

He was agreeing to be interviewed but not for a gentle personality series. He wanted to face the toughest questions possible on the charges he was accused of. He was, in fact, giving me a scoop.

'When?' I asked tentatively, apprehensive that fixing a date might clip the soaring hopes he had just created.

'Tomorrow? Day after? The sooner the better.'

And thus it was that last Saturday I got a chance to question him and the interview you saw was the result.

Now it's not for me to comment on the interview; that would be unethical and uncalled for. Yet I feel I can safely reply to one question I've been repeatedly asked.

Why did he agree? Were those real tears?

Let me start by assuming the emotion was put on. Theoretically it could have been but then Kapil would have to be an actor – not a simple Bollywood product but one of Shakespearean proportions. To cry as he did on demand is not easy. Most of our actors cannot or, at least, not convincingly.

That leads me inexorably to the conclusion that the tears were genuine and the emotion real. I interpret them as the cry of an anguished soul, expressing both pain and helplessness. If you were in his position I think you would behave very similarly. But were they also tears of remorse? I don't think so but, of course, they could have been.

'*Yeh dramebaaz nahin dukhi hein*,' Aru, my secretary, summed up, before softly adding, '*magar samajh nahin aata ki galti kiski thi*?'

8 May 2000

The Eyes that Spoke to Me

It may sound middle-aged but it's very difficult not to be smitten by Madhuri Dixit when you come face to face with her. I was.

We met at Ramoji Film City, Hyderabad. She was there to complete Raj Kumar Santoshi's film *Lajja*. I to interview her. As I approached her room I could feel a frisson of excitement course through my veins. There's something about stars that quickens the flesh. Even past forty you are not immune to it.

I knocked on her door. A man who looked like her dresser opened it. He had a sari neatly folded over his left hand, a bit like a French waiter with a serviette. I announced myself but he remained nonplussed. In his world there was no place for, leave aside recognition of, people like me.

'Madhuriji *hein*?' I asked sounding needlessly tentative but I suppose that was inevitable.

'*Aap kaun*?'

I was about to answer when a voice from inside stopped me.

'Hi,' it trilled. There's really no other word for it. It was cheerful and welcoming. 'Come on in. I've been waiting for you.'

Suddenly introduction seemed superfluous. She knew who I was and I could hardly pretend not to recognize her. As a result my well-planned opening gambit was instantly invalidated. I had intended to start with a 'Hi, I'm Karan Thapar' but now that would sound stupid. In its place all I could come up with was 'Oh, you're ready' and without thinking I said so.

'What did you expect?' Madhuri replied, laughing as she did.

To be honest, I hadn't the faintest idea. I had not meant to say what I had and therefore, I had no idea how to continue. I was, you see, star-struck and a little tongue-tied. After all, what do you say if you come into contact with Sophia Loren, Elizabeth Taylor or even Meryl Streep? If 'Hi, I'm Karan Thapar' is no longer necessary and there's no point in asking, 'Excuse me, are you Elizabeth Taylor?', what do you say instead?

Once again, Madhuri saved the situation. She spoke first and broke the silence.

'I don't know if I'm making a terrible mistake,' she began with a warm but contradictory smile playing about her lips. And then she asked with mischief in her eyes: 'Are you going to eat me up?'

It wasn't a question looking for an answer. She knew that too. I smiled a little sheepishly. In return she gave me the first of her famous looks.

Over the next few hours I saw that look several times and on each occasion it was to beguile me. Even today I can see it clearly in my mind's eye. It is, in fact, my memory of Madhuri. It's also the secret of her charm. The reason why white-haired middle-aged men like me – who clearly should know better – end up hopelessly infatuated.

The famous look is a combination of a smile with the simultaneous movement of her eyes. In fact, not just her eyes but her eyebrows too. The result is that long before Madhuri's voice speaks her face communicates with you. Usually they say the same thing but just sometimes they can speak differently too.

'As the baby of the family, were you spoilt?' I asked. She smiled. Her face gave one answer. Her eyes flashed another. Her laugh conveyed it was the eyes I should go by.

'Ummmm,' her voice exclaimed when I asked if it was love at first sight with Shriram Nene. She was reluctant to answer verbally.

Her eyes, however, were far more eloquent. They had a look that clearly suggested, 'what do you think?'

But it was when I asked if she was really an introvert that the answer from her eyes and that spoken by her mouth were most at odds with each other. 'I am,' her lips said. Her eyes laughed and twinkled with knowing mischievousness. The more her voice pleaded shyness, the more her eyes seemed to ask. 'Do you really believe that?'

The interview over, I realized I wasn't the only one to be hypnotized by her eyes. An enormous crew of seventeen had crammed onto the little set to watch the interview. Each and every one of them had spent the time transfixed by Madhuri's talking eyes.

'*Aankhe dekhi*?' I was asked by our cameraman. Later, most of the others were to ask similar questions too. The funny thing is each of us thought we had noticed something special. Something the next man had not discovered for himself. That's the real magic of Madhuri's eyes. They speak individually even when she is surrounded by a crowd.

Mona Lisa has eyes like that. Look at any of her pictures from any angle and she seems to be looking back straight at you. But hers remain mysterious, even inscrutable, and ultimately silent. Madhuri's are talkative and they speak volumes. I'd like to believe that last week they were talking to me.

4 September 2000

Chapter 12

Cross-border Appeal

'Yaar, aaj mein siraf cigarette *hi pilaunga.'*

A General Lesson

I have to admit, I've never come across someone like Pervez Musharraf. This is not necessarily a compliment. It's simply a statement of fact. But think about it – he's a former dictator who revels in free speech much like a dedicated democrat; he's a general who is, amazingly enough, also a gripping orator; he's a stern disciplinarian but he has a winning sense of humour; he projects a tough commando exterior but his clothes reveal a sharp sense of sartorial elegance. Indeed, he's a man of so many apparent paradoxes, he's impossible to define.

Last Saturday, as he held the India Today Conclave spellbound for over two and a half hours, my mind jumped to our own politicians and I couldn't help compare Musharraf to them. Would Manmohan Singh and Sonia Gandhi or L.K. Advani and Prakash Karat willingly submit themselves to such hostile questioning from an Indian audience and emerge both unscathed and with their *amour propre* intact? The question answers itself. Yet Musharraf has done just that but with one critical difference. The audience – the lions,' den – he faced was not his compatriots but Indians, who could be more accurately described as his enemies.

In contrast, it's not just impossible to picture Manmohan Singh or Sonia Gandhi addressing 500 Pakistanis in the banquet hall of the Marriot in Islamabad; the fact of the matter is they are not even prepared to visit the country. And I would hate to think what could happen if they were questioned the way Musharraf was. Perish the thought!

However, the truth is Musharraf illustrates a deeper difference between India and Pakistan. Pakistanis make themselves accessible to us – be it phone-in interviews on television, formal addresses at conclaves and conferences or simply informal off-the-record chats. We, on the other hand, avoid such encounters like the plague.

It's not simply that Pakistani politicians don't hesitate to give Indians interviews. It's also the sheer number of them. Musharraf, alone, probably gave half a dozen. Prannoy Roy and I got two each. Both he and Asif Zardari have addressed large gatherings in India by live satellite whilst in office and Benazir Bhutto was a frequent visitor and a favourite of our news channels. I don't think there is even one she said no to. In fact, on one particular occasion she gave Aaj Tak two on the same day because the interviewer lost the tapes within minutes of obtaining the first!

In contrast, with the exception of L.K. Advani, I don't think a single leading Indian politician has given the Pakistani media an interview. In fact, I'm prepared to bet that most would not even be prepared to meet them! Again, Advani is the exception.

However, Musharraf exemplifies a further quality our politicians would do well to emulate. He's prepared to face up to his critics, take their hostile questions and spend hours defending his position whilst attempting to change theirs. We may not agree with his arguments and often we disapprove of his tough language but it's impossible not to admire his courage and be impressed by his performance. You may walk away from a Musharraf encounter put off by his personality but, despite that, you also know you've just met a very special man. That's why Musharraf has fans in India and not just foes.

Sadly, many of our politicians refuse to face their critics. Indeed, some can even run away from their friends! The problem is they're not prepared to pit their arguments against challenges. So rarely, if ever, do we see them under pressure, fighting to prove their point, fending off counter-arguments and winning respect for standing their ground.

Yet the paradox is politicians usually grow from such encounters. Musharraf did and still does. But if you shelter yourself from them you appear bonsai and shrunken. That's why ours lose out.

9 March 2009

Two Faces of Pakistan

If I ever needed proof that luck was essential for a television interviewer, this week I got it in abundance. Two interviewees I have pursued with diligence, but not much success, accepted and granted interviews within three days of each other. It turned out to be the right time to talk to both.

The first thing that struck me about Benazir Bhutto and Nawaz Sharif is how different they are. On screen he comes across as genial, even friendly; she seems stern, often forbidding. At times he fumbles, his arguments meander and you feel he's crafting his answers as he replies. She's always assured, her flow unstoppable, her answers planned and when she does expand it's to stop you interrupting.

Nawaz kept a large Pakistani flag by his side, Benazir a small photograph of her late father. His advisors and senior officials crammed into the room to witness the recording. She was on her own and when our cameraman told her staff they were in danger of creeping into the frame she asked them to leave.

She kept her head covered though her dupatta kept slipping off. In his case I felt he wanted to show off the new head of hair he's acquired. Every now and then he would lovingly pat it, no doubt to reassure himself it was still there.

A stark difference was their attitude to Musharraf. Both referred to him as a dictator but thereafter the divergence was vast. Nawaz Sharif refused to accept anything Musharraf has done, including progress on the Kashmir front. Benazir made a point of saying she would not reverse good work even if done by a dictator. Nawaz said he would set up a Kargil Commission and it would be free to question, even try, Musharraf. 'No one is above the law,' he added. Benazir, on the other hand, whilst accepting the need for such a commission, forcefully added that it would not be 'designed for revenge.'

More significant were the differences in their attitude to Kashmir. Both saw it as the core issue – but whilst Nawaz seemed to stick to the UN resolutions as the basis for a solution, Benazir insisted that a solution of the Kashmir issue should not hold up progress in other areas. More importantly, Benazir agrees with the way India and Pakistan are inching towards joint consultative mechanisms. Nawaz, I suspect, either hasn't made up his mind or doesn't like the idea because it's identified with Musharraf.

On militant training camps, access to Hafiz Mohammed Sayeed and Masood Azhar and the extradition of Dawood Ibrahim, I felt they answered with different audiences in mind. Nawaz, no doubt, condemned terrorism but saw it as 'tit for tat.' Both sides need to stop it, he said. He insisted he wouldn't comment on Sayeed or Azhar till he's seen the facts and evaded the Dawood question on the grounds that he ought not to discuss specifics. The audience he was addressing seemed to be in Lahore.

Benazir had no hesitation being forthright. Training camps, if they exist, will be closed down; India's case for access to Sayeed and Azhar would be sympathetically examined; and Dawood could be extradited. I can't say there weren't qualifying clauses in her answers but they were not the bits you remembered. Her message was clear. And it was a message for Delhi.

There was, of course, one area of similarity – they dislike each other with a passion that is uncannily the same. If Nawaz feels let down by Benazir, 'dismayed and disappointed' as he put it, chiding her for cutting a deal with a dictator, she's contemptuous of him. 'I'm more popular,' she interrupted when asked if Nawaz had stolen a march. Nawaz, she insisted, had lived in luxury after accepting exile whilst her husband, Asif, had spent eight years in jail refusing similar leniency.

So what do I make of them? She's tough and cold. He's soft and waffly. If as a viewer you warm to him, equally, you will respect Benazir. It all depends on what you're looking for – likeability or strength.

13 September 2007

The Charm of Pakistani Dictators

I wonder if you realize that Pakistan can boast of a strange but unique tradition? It's produced some of the most charming dictators the world has known! I haven't the faintest idea why this should be the case but, indubitably, it is. Last week as General Musharraf, in his debonair suit and ringing voice, regaled the world it suddenly struck me that he's the third in a line that goes back fifty years.

The first was Field Marshal Ayub Khan. Although he bestowed the rank upon himself, he had the charm and grace of an Englishman. Rajeshwar Dayal, one of our earlier high commissioners, recounts a delightful story that captures the spirit of Ayub. One Ramzan, Dayal was required to urgently call on the president – as Ayub was – to convey a message from New Delhi. He was summoned to Army House at 6.30 in the evening and ushered into the garden where Ayub was sitting admiring the sunset over the Margala Hills.

'Good to see you, Rajeshwar,' the army dictator greeted him. 'What will be your poison?'

Conscious that it was Ramzan and not wanting to offend Ayub's sensitivities, Dayal asked for *nimboo paani.* Ayub looked at him aghast.

'Don't be ridiculous, old chap. Have a decent whisky'.

'But it's Ramzan, Sir,' Rajeshwar spluttered.

'So what?' shot back the field marshal. 'Stop being a good Hindu and become a good Muslim instead!'

Rajeshwar Dayal ends this anecdote with the comment that a couple of Scotches ensured his mission was accomplished most amicably.

Alas, I never met Ayub although I heard a lot about him from my father. If I'm not mistaken, they were almost contemporaries. But I did get to meet the other two dictators. And they were no less charming.

It was in 1985 that I interviewed General Zia-ul-Haq. He was at the very apogee of his power. In those days it was commonplace to remark that he looked like the British comedian Terry Thomas. And certainly the general had a Cheshire Cat-like grin. But his manners were impeccable.

The interview over, General Zia accompanied me out of the drawing room of Army House, down the corridor and to the porch. My car had already driven up. As we spoke, the general reached out and opened the door. With a last handshake and an invitation to return again, he bid me goodbye.

In those days Army House in Rawalpindi had a large circular garden at the front. As the car drove around it and straightened for the final approach to the gate, the general's ADC, who was sitting beside the driver, spoke out.

'Turn around, Mr Thapar, the general's waving goodbye.'

I swivelled in the backseat to find General Zia waving from the porch. As I waved back his hand suddenly moved to his forehead and he gave me a cracking salute.

I was twenty-nine and, no doubt, impressionable but it was hugely flattering – actually thrilling – to be sent off in this style. Later I discovered General Zia did it for every single foreign journalist and they all fell for it like nine pins. It was a ploy, but a very effective one.

General Musharraf is, of course, more matey. There's less ceremony about him. He's more direct, informal and often fairly tactile. He laughs easily and he laughs a lot. The occasion I remember happened in February 2000, four months after he seized power.

We had just finished an hour-long and fairly aggressive interview. It was a bruising experience for both sides. But afterwards, over tea and snacks, he couldn't have been more friendly. Noticing the crew on their own he walked up to engage them in conversation.

Musharraf started by placing an avuncular hand on the cameraman's shoulder. Then, taking out his cigarettes, he offered him one. Nirmal immediately accepted. But when it came to Bunty's turn, our sound recordist replied: 'Sir, *mein* cigarette *nahin peeta*.'

The general chuckled and winked. '*Yaar, aaj mein siraf* cigarette *hi pilaunga*!' The allusion was obvious and everyone burst out laughing. General Musharraf had won over my crew.

These are just three little stories but they happened with extraordinary men. Each of them was a dictator. Each Pakistani. And each is proof of how charming they can be. Is this just a coincidence? Perhaps. But would you have said the same of General Pinochet, General Galtieri or even General Franco? Of course, it's true of our own Field Marshal Manekshaw. But then he never became a dictator!

28 September 2006

The Man in a Bib

It was his nickname that first alerted me to the fact that Pakistan's foreign minister is a rather special politician. In Islamabad they call him the five-piece man. It's an affectionate reference to his immaculate suits. Even in the heat of summer he wears a waistcoat. The other two pieces are his matching tie and kerchief. So when he walked into his office last Sunday afternoon for an interview for SAB TV I knew what to expect. What I had not anticipated was that he can cut quite a dash.

'Look out for his ties,' I had been advised by one of his officials. 'He's very fond of them and they're always striking.'

The tip was accurate. Last weekend the tie was burnt-ochre, a striking contrast with his navy-blue suit. But it was his cufflinks that actually caught my eye. Made of gold, they were set with a row of diamonds at one corner and a large ruby at the other. They weren't discreet but nor were they distasteful.

But there was more to his apparel than immediately met the eye. Underneath the waistcoat he had on black silk braces. It's an old-fashioned touch most natty dressers have dispensed with. I caught a peek when they slid out from under his waistcoat shoulder. If my guess is right I'd say they were Ferragamo.

As Mr Kasuri settled into his armchair I found myself warming to the man.

'I'm sorry to have kept you waiting,' he said gently rubbing his manicured hands. 'I only got back at 3 in the morning from Tehran.'

Most politicians would have refused to give an interview eight hours later. This one was different.

'All right,' he said when I insisted we do the interview the same day. 'But then lunch will have to be afterwards and that could mean it won't happen much before 3.'

I readily agreed. To be honest, I had not expected to be fed. It's never happened before. But the chance of an informal lunch with the Pakistan foreign minister after the proper interview was an invitation no journalist could refuse.

As the cameramen got ready to roll I briefly ran the minister's background through my mind. Kasuri, as his name suggests, comes from Kasur, a part of Pakistani Punjab that borders Firozpur. His father was a lawyer. The son graduated from Cambridge but opted for politics. I know many others with similar pedigrees but few, if any, have fought elections and become ministers. So how does this bird of fine plumage fit into Gen. Musharraf's regime? And what sort of views does he hold? I was soon to discover a second reason why he's a special politician.

Kasuri is a large man. A bit like a teddy bear, if you know what I mean. He keeps his cool and even when provoked he cleverly prefaces his riposte with a warning: 'I did not want to say this but you've left me no option'. The packaging takes the sting out of the reply. It's a clever ploy which allows him to make his point without giving offence. I'm surprised politicians don't use it more often.

Inevitably we talked about cross-border terrorism. He didn't deny it was happening, simply that his government was not behind it. 'We are doing our best to stop it,' he claimed. 'But it's a porous border and despite our efforts some things get through.' He said nine out of ten infiltrators are stopped. The tenth becomes the terrorist we encounter in India.

'This is why talks are so important,' he continued. 'When talks start they will strengthen our hands to tell the Kashmiris to stop.

The talks will offer hope and we can use that to point out that now they don't have to kill themselves. There's another option on offer.'

When I pointed out that Pakistan's handling of Al-Qaeda suspects wanted by Washington was markedly different to those on India's list of twenty, he neither denied the fact nor squirmed with embarrassment. Instead he met the charge head-on.

'Look at the history of tension between our two countries. On the other hand America has been our ally for fifty years. At the moment it's inconceivable that our agencies can share information and work as closely as they do with America. But, Inshallah, that will happen soon.'

Previous Pakistani foreign ministers would have replied very differently. India has not given us any proof, they would have claimed. Or these guys are not in Pakistan. Or even, no formal list has been given. And just as their evasiveness would have hinted at their insincerity, so Kasuri's honesty spoke of his credibility.

At the end of the interview I put to him the doubts we, in India, often express. Men like Kasuri and Prime Minister Jamali may be nice guys but do they count? Power lies with Musharraf and his ministers are only puppets.

The question brought a big smile to his face. I couldn't help think that he looks most like a teddy when he's smiling. But the answer was neither soft nor cuddly.

'The army in Pakistan has a role to play. Our history makes that obvious. But that doesn't mean they run the place and others don't count. And let me tell you the day I cannot agree with the General I'll resign. That may not be a wise thing for a politician to say but it's the truth.'

Afterwards, as we sat down to lunch in the foreign minister's private dining room, he saw me staring at the wine glasses brimming with magenta liquid. He must have fathomed my thoughts.

'Coke,' he laughed, 'but it looks better in those glasses.'

'And the taste?'

'Unfortunately, that stays the same!'

I wasn't the least surprised when he tucked his napkin into his collar. I've often wanted to do the same but never dared. But then my ties can't compete. Of course, the foreign minister was aware that some of his guests were staring at him. After all, a man in a bib is not a common sight. But Kasuri wasn't the least bit self-conscious. I suspect he likes the attention. Most of the time he deserves it too.

3 June 2003

Au Revoir, Ashraf

I was staring absent-mindedly out of the window when a colleague asked a question which sparked off a chain of thoughts. News of Ashraf Qazi's recall had just been announced and although I had anticipated it I was still a little shaken. Even when something is inevitable you hope it won't happen. This was certainly one such occasion.

'Are you upset?' Ashok asked.

I suppose the look on my face gave me away. But until he asked the question I did not realize that this was the emotion inside me. I had not paused to consider how I felt. It seemed irrelevant to the larger events happening outside. But now that Ashok had drawn my attention to my feelings I knew he was right.

Ashraf was a friend I got to know five years ago. Before that I only knew him as Abidah's husband. In fact, on the one previous occasion that we met – in Islamabad in 1989 – he seemed stiff; an impression so wrong its only purpose is to underline how little I knew him before 1997.

Over the last five years we became close friends. I found him warm, supportive, trusting and loyal. He was a *bon viveur*, the soul of dinner parties with a manner that put people instantly at ease. If ever a Pakistani knew how to take the sting out of a tense situation, it was Ashraf. But the nicest thing was that he combined two welcome but contradictory qualities: a sharp intelligence with a delightful appetite for good-natured gossip.

Two years ago he pushed to get me an interview with General

Musharraf. By coincidence we flew to Pakistan together. Ashraf was returning to visit his mother.

'How did it go?' he asked the night it happened.

'Okay,' I replied non-committally. I knew he would not like it but I did not know how to say that. I also knew that the response in India would be different but I did not want to say that either.

Five days after the interview was broadcast, Ashraf returned. The next morning he telephoned.

'You know I thought you'd done me in,' he began but he was laughing. 'My heart sank when I saw the interview. Then I read the *Times of India* and thank God for their silly criticism. I don't agree with them but they may have saved my job!'

Any other high commissioner would have taken the matter far more seriously. It could have broken our friendship. Not Ashraf. We went on to become better and closer friends.

A few months later we spent a weekend together in Dehra Dun and Mussoorie. It was the Doon School's Founder's Day and I thought Ashraf ought to see our best school. We drove down together in his Mitsubishi. On the way back he was determined to see Haridwar and Rishikesh. For a while I lost him in the crowd at Lakshman Jhula but when I found him again he was beaming with delight.

'What's up?' I asked.

'You know that lovely tune we heard in the Mall in Mussoorie? I just bought it.'

'What tune?' I hadn't the faintest idea what he was talking about.

'You're a twit. Wait till I put it on.'

As we drove off, he inserted the tape in the car deck and turned to look at me as it started to play. It was Jagjit Singh's *Ram Dhun*.

'Remember it?'

I could not. I had not heard it as we walked up the Mussoorie

Mall. Yet Ashraf's ears had picked it up. He had liked it and now he had made a point of buying it. We drove back listening to the tape. Each time it ended he would rewind and start again.

Last December, the day I was leaving for a brief new year break in London, Ashraf telephoned at lunch time.

'Let's have a bite together,' he suggested.

'I can't. I'm in a dreadful rush and besides you know I hate lunch.'

'Yes I know. But we may never meet again. The way things are developing I may be gone before you return.'

We spent a couple of hours at the Taj Coffee Shop and I can't remember laughing as much on any other occasion. His heart was heavy because he did not want to leave but no one would have realized that. Initially even I did not. Fortunately on that occasion his fears were mistaken. Not this time. I was the one who first predicted last Friday that his time was up. He instantly agreed.

Yesterday Ashraf went back to Pakistan but I hope it will only be for a short stay. Officially, he's just been recalled. Formally he remains the Pakistan high commissioner to India. I pray our relations improve in time for him to return.

20 May 2002

Chapter 13

Dropping Anchor

'They are making love... on India TV!'

Of Course It's an Act – But Can You See Through It?

There's a question which I am repeatedly asked and which today I shall attempt to answer. It's not always asked as a compliment. More often than not it's a simple but sure kick in the pants. But, whatever the motive, it's a question worth asking and answering.

'When you appear on TV, is it natural or are you acting?'

There are two possible reasons for asking the question. As Aroon Purie often teases – and he is and remains a good friend – 'anchors are frustrated actors' or, as I prefer to see it, anchoring a show is an act in itself. The first is to suggest that anchors are frauds; the second implies that fraudulence is what anchoring is essentially about. So, as I see the dilemma, am I a fraud or is the job I love and like fraudulent? The difference, I admit, may seem slight and possibly insignificant to you. To me it matters an awful lot.

There are three types of answers that I know of. The first, ironically, is from the innocent bystander who recognizes me as an anchor and enthusiastically starts to question. Little does he realize that his question is the answer.

'You always quarrel with the people you interview,' it starts. 'Are you naturally unlikeable or pretending?'

'No,' I usually reply, trying hard to smile and suggest that I am, in fact, full of warmth despite my *rakshas* features.

'Then why do you always sound so quarrelsome?'

To that I have no answer. If how an anchor sounds is to determine whether he or she is putting on an act then all I can add is that the act is a flop. A huge failure. The anchor, in this instance, is a fraud. A horrible fraud. And a very bad actor to boot.

The second answer is only seemingly kinder but behind the gentleness lies a toughness that can hurt if not also damage. I often fall for it till I see the sharp end and usually by then it is too late. Bloodshed – by which I mean my blood – follows.

'The problem with anchors,' this answer begins, 'is that they have to sound as if they mean what they are asking. So even when the question is patently silly the voice behind it is full of conviction and belief.'

Now, on the surface that appears to be a compliment. It's like saying you make the most damned fool question sound credible. The only problem is that the question itself is of your own devising. So, if you are asking it you – and you alone – are responsible for doing so. In fact, the implication is that if you had realized it was a foolish question you wouldn't have asked it in the first place. The fact that you did proves that you too are a fool.

This is the sort of beguiling explanation most anchors usually find themselves initially agreeing with until it is too late. By then it is so self-incriminating that all you can do is smile and slink off.

However, it is the third response that is the most devastating. It floors me each and every time. Actually, that's a euphemism; I'm knocked out by it.

'The problem with interviewers,' this final answer goes, 'is that they are all the same. They are argumentative and they always look aggressive. Why can't you people be less of one or the other? Let the conversation be less argumentative or your manner less aggressive.'

At first hand even I would agree with that. It sounds so

reasonable. So eminently sensible. But if you think about it you'll realize how deeply subversive the comment actually is.

The first suggestion is that interviewers are both argumentative and aggressive by design. Yet the truth is they are not. The second is that their argumentativeness and aggressiveness is put on and can, equally easily, be switched off. But that's not the case and it never could be. The final assumption is that both the person and the job he or she is doing require that argumentativeness and aggressiveness be a part of it. No doubt that could be the case on some occasions but equally there are many when the opposite is also true.

No, the fact of the matter is that some interviews require argumentativeness and aggressiveness and others don't. Which is determined more by the interviewee than the interviewer. To blame the latter for the outcome is a teensy-weensy bit like criticizing the messenger for the message. Of course, we all do but that still doesn't make it right.

So, to return to the original question and to try and answer it personally: am I putting on an act when you see me on the screen? The answer is both yes and no. And that's not being facetious or flippant but the honest truth.

Of course anchors are trying to convey an image. They all do. When they succeed you don't see it as an act because it has worked. When you see through it, it has not. But on both occasions it is a performance. Or else how do you account for the fact that an anchor can interview a friend toughly and carry on as a pal thereafter or be seemingly sympathetic with a person he actually cannot abide and then coldly ignore him once it is over?

Incidentally, writing is also, if not equally, an act. But can you see through it? Try by reading this piece twice!

22 November 1999

Are We Peeping Toms?

These days it's not unusual for the phone to ring at midnight. Although I must admit I was taken aback the first time it happened. It was my colleague Ashok. He never fails to alert me when something unexpected occurs. But even he was uncharacteristically excited.

'Guess what?' he began. It was an odd start to the conversation.

'You tell me,' I replied, trying to be cool and collected.

'They're making love on TV!'

'Who?' I shouted. I'm afraid my voice betrayed my surprise. 'Where?'

'On India TV. Rajat Sharma's channel has tricked some MLAs in Bihar. It's a sting operation and he's showing it no-holds-barred.'

That was enough for me to switch on. For the next forty-five minutes I sat glued to the box. I knew what I was seeing was deplorable but it was also irresistible. I decided to reproach myself in the morning but carry on for now.

It was hazy, unclear and the best bits were covered with a mosaic pattern which made them hard to see. Yet it was obvious what was happening. Poor sods, I said, but kept watching. After a bit it wasn't curiosity or even the 'pornography' value that retained my attention but *schadenfreude* – a sadistic pleasure in other people's misery. I hated myself for it but I could not stop.

A few days later Ashok rang again. Not surprisingly, at midnight.

'Switch on India TV'. But this time he sounded less excited. 'They've done a sting on Shakti Kapoor. The poor chap's been caught trying to seduce a girl who wants to be an actress.'

I watched for half an hour. This time it wasn't someone clandestinely filmed making love but a middle-aged man embarrassing himself as a young siren egged him on. Ashok tells me that India TV plans to similarly expose other Bollywood and television stars. In fact earlier they showed priests at it. I get the feeling it's become part of their weekly schedule; if it's Sunday, it's some luckless fool caught in the act!

I suppose from Rajat Sharma's point of view this is a clever ploy. Behind the claim of good quality investigative journalism he's broadcasting a diet of pornography, *schadenfreude* and famous people tricked into carelessness on camera. For a while, no doubt, people will watch. But the question is how often? And will this win their admiration and respect?

The answer turns on three issues.

First, what do you prove when you show people can be lured by sex? Nothing, except they're just like the rest of us. Offer a man a woman and a chance to make love without obvious risk or a price to pay and most of us would accept. Some might pause a bit, others look over their shoulders, a few ask for reassurance but then, once fear and doubt have been laid to rest, many would say yes. That's what the priests and MLAs did. That's even what Shakti Kapoor thought would happen although, in his case, he seems to have created the opportunity for himself. But are any of them worse than us? In their place might we not have fallen into the same trap? Their problem is not their lapse but that they got caught.

Second, falling for sex is not the same as accepting a bribe. It's weakness of the flesh not proof of moral infirmity. Maybe in a priest it's also hypocrisy but that's hardly a cardinal sin leave aside a crime. And in a Bollywood actor/producer it's probably a necessity.

Third, do these exposes matter? No doubt they're titillating but what do they amount to? We're watching ordinary people who've been tricked into making a display of themselves. Quite frankly, I feel sorry for them. We can all be tempted or trapped into doing something silly and if someone broadcasts it he only shows that we're human. Of course, he also proves he's a monster – and I use the word advisedly!

In fact, I would add a fourth issue. After hours of watching India TV if I'm left thinking of such concerns I can't help feeling I've wasted my time. Would I therefore want to re-visit the channel?

I put that question to Ashok but his reply took my breath away.

'Oh no doubt you will,' he laughed. 'Every time I ring you'll switch on but I can't guarantee for how long.'

Does that mean Rajat has got the better of me? Or is the word better the opposite of what I mean?

17 March 2005

Listen to Yourself!

I often wonder if our media is schizophrenic? On the one hand if you stand back and observe how we respond to situations you'll notice that, more often than not, we jump to extremes. Whether its adulation or criticism, we opt for the hyperbolic. Measured, balanced, judicious, well-considered comment eludes us. A string of adjectives trips off our tongues – or our pens – and then, like children, we start to compete and outdo each other.

Yet the amazing thing is somewhere at the back of our minds – or deep inside our hearts – we know we're overdoing it. Whether its speech or action, we know when we've spoken or done too much. At times we're even capable of stepping outside our skins and commenting on ourselves. Like two different people, we can judge each other yet not stop the errant behaviour.

An email from Vishal Pant, hours after Abhinav Bindra's Olympic gold, captures this Janus-headedness. Writing about the explosion of attention on TV – and anticipating the next day's papers – he says: 'A country of a billion is celebrating as if we have won the maximum golds at the Olympics! I hate to sound like a cynic but I get amazed when I see this kind of reaction. For God's sake even countries like Ethiopia and Surinam have won golds. Hats off to Bindra – a huge achievement – but why are we going beserk?' For my part, I doubt if the American media greeted Phelps' record-breaking tally of golds with similar glee!

The paradox is that Vishal is a senior producer at Times Now, a channel as guilty of going beserk as any other. But Vishal's response would not have been out of place at any of the competitor channels. Each of them has a handful of producers who lament their lack of balance – yet are unable to do anything about it. In fact, not just unable, even unwilling. They know their channels often lack perspective and balance but they accept that, even defend it, whilst admitting its wrong. Now, isn't that schizophrenic?

What surprised was that television anchors were so swept off their feet they failed to recognize Abhinav's modesty. When he responded to that ceaselessly-asked, unimaginative old-chestnut 'how do you feel?' with a gentle reticent 'there's not much to say … for me life will go on', one concluded he was 'blasé' whilst another commented 'he seems to be taking it in his stride.' Tell me, is that such a bizarre thing to do?

Yet the sad part is this extreme response to Abhinav's achievement is a belittling of journalism. If a single gold medal – even if it's the first – can push into the background the crisis in Kashmir, the rising rate of inflation and the cash-for-votes corruption scandal then, surely, we are either a media that has its priorities upside-down or is desperately running away from bigger issues? Either way, that's what you expect of a comic state in a Verdi opera not the world's largest democracy.

But why single out this week's coverage of Abhinav? Was the treatment of the Arushi murder, the Scarlet Keeling rape or the Delhi gay killings any different? In fact, you can find several examples each year stretching all the way back to Ganesh statues drinking milk! Exaggeration is our forté.

I suspect television news channels started this slide into madness. Their competition for eyeballs is in danger of converting journalism from all that you ought to know into all that you want to know and, even, all that you will readily and happily watch. Today, ten years later, our papers have caught up. They've dropped their commitment to high standards. Instead, they're racing down the same low road to cheap popularity and tabloid success.

So, here's my reply to Vishal – and all the others like him, hidden and unheard inside television and newspaper offices: 'India is not going beserk but perhaps you guys in TV and the papers are. It's time for you to do more than SMS. It's time to act. If you don't, you could drive the rest of us insane!'

14 August 2008

In Defence of Politicians

'Poor you! I simply don't know how you stand it.'

It was an odd way to start a conversation and it took me aback.

'Stand what?'

'The politicians you meet and keep interviewing.'

'Why?' I asked, still perplexed. But the lady looked at me as if I was the one who wasn't making sense. She puffed on a long cigarette, blew the smoke stylishly over her shoulder and turned to explain. We were guests at a party last weekend. She was dressed in large white pearls and a transparent skimpy saree. However, I shall be discreet and hold back her name.

'They seem such ghastly people. They come across as selfish, quarrelsome and full of themselves.'

Her vehemence surprised me. Whilst a few politicians may be like that the vast majority are not. Of them my opinion is very different. But that only meant I found myself locked in a long argument. It developed into a regular ding-dong but I'm not sure I convinced her. However, I did realize that television is partly responsible for conveying this false impression. Most of you who don't know politicians judge by the way you see them. But the presentation is neither wholly accurate nor truly fair. Today I want to make amends.

The problem begins with our television talk shows which encourage politicians to quarrel. It's not that left to themselves they would be sedate and calm, reasonable and reflective, but that we've convinced them and probably entrapped them into believing that the fight is more important than the argument. The fault lies in the way such shows are conceived. They seek to portray the *tamasha* of politics – its theatre and spectacle rather than its content and substance. They generate heat but they don't shed light.

Unfortunately most politicians willingly play along. Once the cameras roll they slip into a role, perform to a preconceived script. The result is quarrelsome shouting matches which lead nowhere and are usually an end in themselves.

This is tragic for at least two reasons. Firstly, it demonizes politicians. In fact, it panders to the already widespread opinion that they are a base tribe. People readily accept what they see because it bolsters their already biased view.

More importantly, it wastes politicians. The object of a television talk show is to inform and to learn. This can be done in many ways. By explaining issues, by discussing differing views, by seeking answers, by carefully analysing. But each of these require that we listen and to listen we have to care about what we hear.

That's where our problems start. Channel heads believe audiences don't care about the discussion. They claim most subjects bore them. Worse still, they don't think audiences can be made to listen. In their opinion serious conversation is a switch-off. Rather than risk that they blend it with drama. Create a storm in the studio and the thunder and lightening will hold the audience. It doesn't matter that the atmospherics are simply a waste of time. Or that politicians are used as objects to laugh at rather than people one can learn from.

Fortunately, the solution is simple. It would follow automatically if we change our attitude to news and current affairs. So far we judge these shows by their ratings. We assume they are products for a mass market. But they're not, nor should they be. News, and more so current affairs, are only for those who want to know and, dare I say it, care to. They are not vehicles for delivering eyeballs to advertisers. Yet when they are treated as such it becomes inevitable they will be designed primarily to capture attention. That's why channel heads are scared of demanding concentration and, instead, lure with cacophony.

Yet we have producers, editors, cameramen and even anchors who could comfortably take on the BBC and CNN. We could easily deliver a comparable product for ourselves. The reason we don't is because those who run channels either don't trust the audience or don't know how to differentiate it. They fear that if they make you concentrate you will run away and they don't have the confidence to realize that if you do it won't really matter.

So this is not a case of getting the programmes we deserve. Clearly we deserve better. This is a case of receiving the type of programmes our channel heads think we will accept. The question is: how do you change that?

That's the challenge the lady I met last weekend should address. Unfortunately, that's also the bit of the conversation she found most difficult to follow. But I can confidently predict that if she succeeds she will discover that most politicians are very different to the impression she has of them.

Now, wouldn't that be a pleasant surprise?

31 March 2003

The Press and Punishment

How good is Indian journalism? It's a question the prime minister asked last weekend and in answering pointed out critical, if not damaging, lapses in accuracy and methodology and, most importantly of all, the willingness to take corrective action.

There's no doubt ours is a free press, often though not always fearless, and usually entertaining. But how well informed is it? How reliable? How reflective of India's complex, even conflicting, concerns? And how responsible? Only if the answer to these questions is yes can we claim Indian journalism is good and on par with the best in the world.

Sadly, that's not always the case. As the PM put it, 'In the race for capturing markets, journalists have been encouraged to cut corners, to take chances, to hit and run.' We do stories without checking all the facts or giving ample opportunity to the affected people to answer the charges we're levelling. We accept material from vested interests without hesitation and claim it's reliable. We damage reputations without concern for individuals in the spurious belief there's a greater national interest involved. And we're obsessed with the world of urban glamour and reluctant to look beyond it. Often politicians and businessmen set our agenda. In response we become a part of their *tu tu mein mein* rather than look for the big picture.

However, the nub of the PM's point is the question: 'How many mistakes must a journalist make, how many wrong stories, how many motivated columns before professional clamps are placed?'

It's not an easy one to answer. Certainly journalists must face the consequences when they're wrong. It's a way of guarding against casual carelessness. But what's the appropriate punishment?

For instance, when a well-known TV channel recently claimed Sania Mirza was the first Indian to make it to round four of a grand slam, forgetting that Ramanathan Krishnan had entered the semis at Wimbledon and his son, Ramesh, and Vijay Amritraj had made it to the quarters, it was a mistake which called for a reprimand and a close watch on future work to ensure such carelessness was not repeated. But that's all. Yet when a major business daily based a front page lead story on the claim that the PM had held meetings with SEBI, RBI, CBI and IB to look into the phenomenal rise in Sensex, and it turned out to be completely untrue, it called for sterner measures.

The first error was a result of not knowing enough. The second of not cross-checking 'facts'. Of course, both ignorance and negligence are mistakes but in punishing them you need to ask three questions to determine the response that would fit the lapse: was the error easily avoidable? What consequences did it lead to? And how much damage has it done to the newspaper or TV channel? Then whatever follows must be done impartially and transparently.

More difficult to judge is what the PM calls 'motivated columns'. Who's to decide what's motivation? And who's to decide whether it's acceptable or not? Here the PM is on shaky ground. After all, it could be said every article has a motivation – be it to inform, expose, interpret, analyse, amuse, put in perspective or deliberately play devil's advocate. The problem is one man's motivation is another's provocation and it turns, I suspect, on each individual's predilection. Quite frankly, I think it's best to leave it at that.

But there is an area where the PM needs to look beyond the press to his own tribe of politicians, including his partymen and allies. When he says 'the media must play its due rule in influencing public opinion so that liberal values are reinforced', he's right but he's also overlooking the fact it usually does. It's politicians who often don't. Last week when Khushboo was forced to recant her comments on the unimportance of virginity it was under alleged pressure from the PMK and its supporters. The press stood by her. Dr Manmohan Singh's allies did not.

And what about politicians who use their muscle to coerce journalists to write or recant to suit their tastes? Of course, the journalist cannot escape blame when it happens but what about the politician or the political party? Are they not equally to blame? At least I think so.

Perhaps the PM should have addressed a carefully crafted sentence or two to them. It would have ensured that his critique of the media would have been widely accepted without reservation.

29 September 2005